Living with Consciousness

Everyday Inspirations for Spiritual Growth and Personal Fulfillment

Nozer Kanga

Copyright © 2018 by Nozer Kanga
All rights reserved. No part of this book, in part or in whole, may be reproduced, transmitted or utilized in any form or by any means, electronic, photographic or mechanical, including photocopying, recording or by any information storage and retrieval system without prior permission from the author-publisher.

ISBN: 1981958304
ISBN 13: 9781981958306
Library of Congress Control Number: 2017919697
CreateSpace Independent Publishing Platform
North Charleston, South Carolina

For my wife, Dinaz. You have brought a new meaning to my life; for that I am ever grateful. For my sons, Dennis, Freddy, and Vishtasp. You all are an inspiration to me and I look forward to the next day to enjoy my meaningful journey in life.

I love you all.

Nozer

Table of Contents

Preface vii

1	The Journey Forward	1
2	The Energies That Define Us	7
3	Managing Positive and Negative Energies	30
4	Karma—the Universal Law	45
5	Spiritual Learning and Soul Development	56
6	Our Relationships, Our Selves	72
7	Our Spiritual Trainers	88
8	Earthly Power and the Power Within	99
9	Spiritual Truths and Individual Truth	118
10	Life and the Benefits of Purposeful Living	129
11	Coping with Life's Challenges	149
12	One Universal God	170
13	The Soul	181
14	Uplifting and Transforming Our Souls	200
15	Raising and Shifting Consciousness	208

Suggested Reading 225
Author Biography 227

Preface

LIVING WITH CONSCIOUSNESS is a product of my life's journey on Earth. When I was young, I never understood the meaning of consciousness; nor did I understand the purpose of my earthly existence, or why I was encountering certain individuals in life who were sources of grief, unhappiness, and suffering. I was caught in that cycle for a long time until, in 1985, I met Khorshed and Rumi Bhavnagri, who helped me understand the reason for my existence on Earth and why I had to go through certain tests and training in life.

Over the years I have read many spiritual books but the principal basis of my learning has been *The Laws of the Spirit World*, (Jaico Publishing House, 2009) written by Khorshed Bhavnagri. Khorshed was a spiritual teacher and dearest friend who did not hesitate to correct me on my spiritual faults. She used to hold spiritual classes in Bombay (Mumbai) and Canada, which my wife and I were blessed to attend. Her classes were simple and taught us about the existence of God and the law of karma, and how to lead our lives on Earth, build relationships, go through our tests and training peacefully, and raise our spiritual consciousness. Each class had a different theme. Each topic touched our heart and soul, and each topic made us realize that we were born to help and serve others in life.

During my life, I have come to understand that, in order to change spiritually, we each need to elevate our individual consciousness. In this way, we gain the ability to look at things from a different perspective, to embrace our spiritual tests and training, and to experience our earthly journey with peace and joy.

I have always known that God has a plan for everyone, a divine purpose. In the universe as a whole, we are each a piece of the puzzle. When things don't work out the way we want, there is nonetheless a higher spiritual meaning, a meaning we cannot understand when we allow turmoil to control our lives. But when we listen to our higher selves we gain clarity, and our lives become more creative and meaningful.

This book describes my life, my journey, and the earthly and spiritual experiences that have guided and benefitted me. Each earthly experience shaped the way I lead my life today and made me realize that we are born to assist and serve others. Until we do so, our journey is neither promising nor fulfilling. In my lifetime, I have been required to undergo certain challenging earthly experiences so that I could learn, grow, and evolve spiritually. Once I acquired the art of learning from my journey on Earth, it was easy for me to accept whatever difficulties I encountered and to apply my spiritual learning to my life.

In the course of my journey, many types of people—including friends, my children, and colleagues—have taught me something meaningful. My friends showed me the path of loyalty and honesty. My children taught me how to control my temper and cultivate patience. My colleagues taught me the path of commitment, and some even showed me the effects of betrayal. The people I have encountered have impacted my life in varying ways. In some cases, they were just passersby—friends and colleagues whose journeys I observed. Certain other people, however, had such a profound impact on me and my life that I was able to see clearly the reason for my being born on Earth.

Over the years, I have learnt that we can only promote change in others when we each raise our own consciousness and see things from a higher perspective. Anger, irritation, impatience, and frustration lead us nowhere. Such feelings impair the ability to focus and harm the spirit, which in turn creates disruption, discord, and disharmony in our work and personal lives. The joy of living is to exist in peace and harmony. I have always loved the proverb "Live and let live" but I can add five more words: "Live and let others live in peace and harmony." In whatever capacity we live and lead, we have the power to change the lives of others, including our families, friends, colleagues, and indeed everyone with whom we directly and indirectly come into contact. How we use our energies, truth, power, authority, flexibility, knowledge, and wisdom is entirely in our own hands. We each have the ability to create a better environment that will encourage other people to connect with us and share their pain, suffering, joy, and triumphs.

Individuals possess different levels of consciousness. Some have strong, positive, and dominant spiritual qualities, whereas others might demonstrate less spiritual development. Even though we possess different levels of consciousness, we are all connected on Earth through soul consciousness. And each of us has the power to change our individual consciousness. The way to change lies in using our energies and power productively, through positive thoughts, positive words, and positive actions; in building harmonious relationships with one another; and in performing acts of kindness. Overall, to change is to go through life's journey on Earth while accepting all spiritual tests and training that we encounter. In the end, this acceptance is the path to higher consciousness.

I hope that you will find this book inspiring to read and that my experience will provide you with strategies for your own lives. At the end of each chapter, I have provided summarizing points to further guide you in your journey. It is my sincerest wish that these signposts or, as I call them, *inspirational connections* will bring you clarity as you fulfill your life's purpose.

In my lifetime I have discovered the importance of making a determined effort to gain self-understanding and to make desired personal changes. In this way, we each reap rewards for ourselves, our spirits, and the people who surround us in our daily lives.

With love,
God bless.
Nozer

1
The Journey Forward

The road of life twists and turns and no two directions are ever the same. Yet our lessons come from the journey, not the destination.

—Don Williams Jr.

INNUMERABLE TIMES, I have asked myself, why was I born on Earth and what is the purpose for my existence? Each time I asked these questions, I received only one answer from the higher mind. *You are special.* You are here to learn and to grow spiritually and to make a meaningful contribution in this universe. Your journey is in your hands and the choices you will make over the course of your life will shape your destiny in the future. This answer was inspiring but it took me a while to understand the laws of the universe, the reason for my existence, and why I was encountering people and circumstances that put me at the centre of grief and on the receiving end of certain life-challenging situations.

I often could not help questioning why things were not going right in my life. Why me? What did I do to deserve this treatment? Is life fair? I asked myself day and night. When I had developed the correct spiritual understanding, my higher mind told me that we need to accept all life challenges with a smile, that each and every person who comes into our lives—whether bringing grief or happiness—helps us to grow spiritually and advance in consciousness.

Have you ever thought about why you were born on Earth? Do you know your life's purpose? Are you happy with your life? Is your life meaningful? Do you enjoy your journey on Earth? Do you want to bring a spiritual meaning into your life and work? Do you want to achieve inner peace and happiness, or do you want to achieve fame, recognition, and glory at the expense of others? These are big questions and finding meaningful answers to them might seem to be virtually impossible. But in fact, every single day, the answers are right in front of us.

The Importance of Each Day

Our journey on Earth is in many ways an everyday matter; it is the journey of normal human beings going about their business on Earth. How we each start the day is important in all facets of life, whether we are managing, leading, directing, or supervising people; staying at home raising children; or performing clerical or manual jobs. So, how *do* we start the day? Are we starting with peace and positivity? Are we centred and aligned in mind, body, and spirit? What are the thoughts that run through our minds when we wake up?

Though we might all participate in some sort of collective soul consciousness, we do not all share one mind at the level of the everyday. As individuals, we can make choices. Do we wake up with positive thoughts and the intention of making a difference in the lives of others (family, friends, children, employees, teams, departments, bosses, and customers)? Or do we wake up with a notion of hurting, harming, or humiliating someone in life? How we individually answer these last two questions indicates how we are leading our lives and what is causing us grief, anger, stress, anxiety, illness, and unhappiness. We are each the source of our own inner happiness. If we are miserable, we have no one to blame but ourselves.

In today's world, people get recognized by their power, material wealth, status, and other aspects of external appearances. We fail to see the real person's soul and to appreciate that someone who does not have wealth, status, power, or prestige might have a highly developed spiritual life. That person has more than many others to offer in terms of kindness, honesty, lovingness, compassion, and humility. Characteristics such as these are crucial for leading a healthy spiritual life. Society, however, does not always recognize spiritually aware people, and such people typically do not want to be recognized.

In order to achieve fame, glory, power, and other earthly objectives, we make unconscious choices in life—choices that impact and hamper our own spirits. Sometimes these choices are made in haste out of thoughtlessness, or sometimes for selfish needs and gains. How we continuously make conscious and unconscious choices is at the heart of both our day-to-day and spiritual lives. For the well-being of both, we can each use our individual truth, power, and will to make conscious choices that will generate positive energy and feelings of joy and happiness in the lives of others. Sometimes I feel sad knowing that, instead of helping our fellow human beings and bringing joy into the lives of others, we are sometimes instruments for creating hate and resentment in others because of our own unconscious actions. Our role on Earth should be to create joy and peace for others in life.

To begin to grasp our true purpose in life, we must ask ourselves some profound questions: Are we doing the right thing? Are we moving in the right spiritual direction and building our spiritual connection with God and universe? Are we happy from within? Do we feel content, inspired, and loving? Or are we disconnected in mind, body, and spirit? And has daily life lost its charm and meaning?

If you answered yes to the last two questions, the situation is not as difficult to remedy as you might think. The way forward is to set your sights on the basics of everyday living and to begin at the beginning. The first step is simply to start each day with the right attitude.

Making a Good Start

From the moment of awakening, the basic foundation for starting a good, inspiring day is to cultivate positive, pure, honest, and selfless thoughts. We each need to start the day with the goal of bringing a smile to someone else's face; each morning we need to connect with our higher selves and ask for an opportunity to serve others during the day. This is the simplest of the simple steps that give us the power to perform with true and clear intentions.

This is always the first help I seek from God when I wake up in the morning.

Gratitude is another important aspect of beginning a productive day. A short, sincere prayer to thank God for the wonderful opportunities that lie ahead will help you reach the workplace in a pleasant mood, whether you commute a long distance or walk a few paces to your home office.

The Rewards of Change
If we are willing to make changes in our lives, we will find opportunities abounding to help others in one way or another. These opportunities will be endless. The more we help others, the more we want to help others. When we focus our attention on others, and for others, the journey that we each make becomes fulfilling, and inspiring.

• • •

Inspirational Connections

- You are special.
- Your life's purpose is to grow spiritually and to contribute to the universe by helping others.
- Everyone you meet can teach you something to take your journey forward.
- You are the source of both your own misery and your own happiness.
- Start each day with positive intentions by connecting to your higher self and asking for an opportunity to make life better for others.
- Willingness to change is the first step forward.

2
The Energies That Define Us

*Taking the first footstep with a good thought,
the second with a good word, and the third
with a good deed, I entered paradise.*

—*Zoroaster*

WE LIVE TOGETHER in a world of energy. Each one of us constantly produces energy through our thoughts, words, and actions—a commonalty that all human beings share. Just as our physical bodies need energy to perform all our day-to-day activities, our souls need energy to survive spiritually. Spiritual energy is the source that connects all our souls in our day-to-day lives.

We can observe and measure our physical energy based on the daily work we complete, or the number of hours we work out in the gym, or on any other activity we perform without getting tired or drained. Spiritual energy, however, is not so readily grasped. Such energy is formless, cannot be seen with our naked eyes, and changes every minute according to our thoughts, words, and actions. It is further affected by how we internally feel about our own selves and externally react to others.

Depending on a person's state of mind, the energy produced is either positive or negative. When our thoughts, words, and deeds are positive, we create positive energy. Similarly, when our thoughts, words, and actions are negative, we generate negative energy for ourselves, for the people around us, and for the environment.

> Positive thoughts, words, and actions → create positive feelings.
> Positive feelings → generate positive energy.
>
> Negative thoughts, words, and actions → create negative feelings.
> Negative feelings → generate negative energy.

Energy and the Soul

Energy is the fuel for our souls. A soul on a high frequency will most of the time run on positive energy, while a soul on a low frequency chugs along on negative energy. This correlates to the simple principle that thoughts (mind), words (body) and actions (spirit) produce positive or negative energy.

A person operating at a high frequency focuses mainly on the positive aspects of self and others, which in turn radiates positive energy and is healing to the soul, to individual and collective consciousness, and to the environment. Positive energy radiates brightness and light—it creates feelings of love and harmony. It is a force that can heal illnesses and ensure peace of mind. Positive energy seeps through one soul to another and the effect multiplies.

People on lower frequencies create the reverse effect because they are constantly directing negative thoughts at themselves and at others. They often indulge in self-pity, jealousy, anger, hatred, and thoughts of revenge. For them, the positive is at best a distant beacon. Its light does not exist at a soul level or, if it does, they do not listen to their higher minds telling them to take the right actions in life.

Negative energy remains enshrouded in dullness and darkness; it creates an imbalance in the environment and the result is neither peaceful nor in harmony with nature. Constant negative energy diminishes the spirit as well as the soul. Compared to positive souls, the soul caught in negativity is dim and lacks either transparency or authenticity. The word *service* do not seem to exist in the vocabulary of negative souls. Selflessness does not exist at any level in such souls, and the outcomes they seek are typically negative.

We human beings have the tendency to absorb or repel positive and negative energy depending on the development of our souls. A soul with a higher consciousness absorbs positive energy and repels negative energy, while a soul with a lower consciousness takes in negative energy faster and resists positive energy. To change our energy level, we each need to change how we lead our life and structure our consciousness. We can start by striving to become pure in our thoughts, words, and actions. Once we take this step, it will become a routine, and we will always generate positive energy that will be beneficial for us, our souls, and the people and environment around us. Our energy never dies. When our bodies cease to breathe, the energy level we possessed on the earthly plane passes into the spirit world, and the soul ends up in the realm suitable to the individual's energy level. It is therefore important to remember that while we are on Earth, our individual energy can evolve. Whether it does so in a positive or negative direction depends on our intentions. Are they noble and selfless—or manipulative and selfish?

Each intention has a positive or a negative energy associated with it. When we turn intention into thoughts, words, or actions, the result is either a high- or a low-frequency energy. In other words, the flow of energy in the universe is such that our own thoughts, words, and actions have meaning not only to each of us as a human being on Earth but also as a soul with a continuing existence. We can thus shape our own destinies by raising our awareness of what we think, say, and do.

Flow of Energy—Positive Thoughts

Thoughts are powerful generators of energy. Our physical minds produce thoughts based on our perception of others and the world around us. If our perception is favourable, we generate positive thoughts, and if our perception is cynical and judgmental, we generate negative thoughts. Henry David Thoreau (1817–1862) has rightly said, "Thought is the sculptor who can create the person you want to be."

Our physical minds are so active that we are constantly thinking about a pleasant experience or a problem in the past or about how the future will unfold in our lives. Often, because we live in a materialistic world, our physical minds are preoccupied with current situations and all their accompanying worries.

When we direct our thoughts in a positive direction, we sense the infinite power in the universe and feel that nothing is going to hamper our spirit and progress, as the universe will provide us with all the right possibilities in life. Positive thoughts strengthen the connection of mind, body, and spirit. We are in harmony with nature and our true selves. We feel energized, connected to the universe, and assured that its power will guide us toward the right path in life.

On the other hand, when we focus on the negative aspects of ourselves or others, we tend to push positive thoughts into the background, granting our physical mind licence to germinate negative thoughts. As a result, we feel discouraged, disheartened, disappointed, and angry as we wander, lost, in the maze of negativity. The unproductive energy produced is self-perpetuating, and it takes a lot of positive energy and willpower to snap out of the pattern of negative thinking.

During the hours, or sometimes days, that we spend in the negative zone, we can adversely affect other people. Even if we don't actually say or do anything objectionable, we are to some extent impacting the energy of others and hindering our own spiritual progress. When we have negative thoughts about another person, our positive energy is depleted and we create an unwholesome environment for the mind, body, and spirit. The resultant sense of hopelessness not only infects us and our own lives but spreads to others who are in contact with us and to the surroundings in which we coexist. As humans, we are always susceptible to negative thoughts—the root causes of which are fear, doubt, and lack of self-confidence. We often do not have faith in God and harbour doubts that God will do what is best for us in our lives. If, however, we were to remove all doubt and fear, and replace these with faith in God, it would be a welcome change for the human soul and spirit.

Fortunately, we each have the power to relinquish our negative thoughts and to focus on what is good and positive. The key is to change our view of others and the world. The moment that we shift our perceptions from negative to positive, the universe creates a comparable reaction in other people, who in turn shift their own thoughts toward the positive. The universe then balances thoughts and energy to create a unified, harmonious environment.

Thought alone has no form or substance but it is nonetheless the basic mechanism for transforming perceptions and intentions into words and actions. If our thoughts are pure, we will always express pure, positive, and meaningful words to other people. If our thoughts are negative, we will always express impure, nasty, spiteful words for the other person. A mere thought can also generate a negative feeling for another person and distance us from others. We should constantly be aware of our thoughts and keep them in control.

If thought is the mechanism to generate pure or impure words, it is also the catalyst for the actions we take in life. A positive thought will always allow us to perform acts that are selfless, meaningful, and beneficial to other people and the universe. All too often, the reverse will also be true. Unchecked negative thoughts can lead to selfish, vindictive, spiteful, revengeful, angry, and ego-driven acts.

When we think positively, we are perceiving an outcome that is favourable; similarly, when we think negatively, we are envisioning an unpleasant outcome. Depending on the level of our consciousness, we can take charge of our physical minds and reduce the negative thoughts, or we can keep on feeding the negativity to the point of bringing destruction to ourselves and others. When discord and misalignment dominate mind, body, and spirit, it takes a life-changing learning experience to get back on the right path. The trick is to shift our thought pattern to focus on something positive. We need to cultivate gratitude for what we have in life and to perceive the good in other people and the merits of each of our situations in life. We also need to start thinking and believing that whatever has happened in our lives has happened for our own spiritual growth, that we were meant to go through trials to attain higher consciousness, both individually and collectively. If we hold true to this belief, the universe will find a perfect solution for ourselves and our problems.

Spirituality only works in two ways. Either we will freely make the switch, change, and become positive, or we will be forced to change due to the circumstances that surround us in life. That is why we struggle. We are resisting the very change that is for our own good. The body and soul cannot live in misalignment for a long period of time. We must not, therefore, let the physical mind wander here and there in all directions. But controlling the physical mind is not easy.

Negative thoughts are driven by ego, which is looking for justification, quarrels, proof, the need to be right in all circumstances, and the desire to feel loved and valued at any cost. We can gain control of our egos by making a conscious effort to focus on good and positive thoughts. The moment that we discard a negative thought, our ego loses its hold and the power of negativity diminishes.

Once we shift from negative to positive, we have to keep our minds focused in that direction and move ahead with positive thoughts. If we adhere to this practice, it becomes easier to control our negative thoughts. The more we practice, the less time it will take to switch from the negative and to maintain a positive attitude. A mind filled with positive thoughts generates creativity, inspiration, and happiness, all of which help us lead a healthy life on Earth.

The first two verses of the *Dhammapada*, a collection of sayings by the Buddha, capture the gist of what we need to take to heart in our efforts to master how we think:

> Our life is shaped by our mind; we become what we think. Suffering follows an evil thought as the wheels of a cart follow the oxen that draws it.

> Our life is shaped by our mind; we become what we think. Joy follows a pure thought like a shadow that never leaves. (*The Dhammapada*, introduced and translated by Eknath Eswaran [Blue Mountain Center of Meditation, 2007].)

In other words, what we go through in life is a result of our own thoughts. Evil (negative) thoughts bring misfortune and pain into our lives. Pure (positive) thoughts lead to good fortune and happiness.

Controlling Our Thoughts

We need to keep our intentions and thoughts pure always. When we control our thoughts, we control our words and actions. Thoughts are like seeds. If we water a seed, it grows and blooms into a plant. If we don't water a seed, it will not grow and it will die and disintegrate into the earth. Similarly, if we do not nurture, do not dwell upon, our negative thoughts, they will wither and die. This is the simplest way to control our thoughts.

Some people cannot control the thoughts in their physical minds and thus tend to voice their opinions on any topic or to lash out at others. Some do not speak out loud but carry on a silent dialogue in their minds. The dialogue is like a movie for which the individual is the producer, creator, writer, and observer. To some, this movie will bring pleasure, because what they cannot do in the earthly world they can perform in their physical minds and get away with it. Some play games of winning, revenge, cunning, and manipulation; some even play the game of killing another person. Like a virtual game, such mind games bring pleasure, but there is also a crucial difference: mind games are thoughts—realities that can disrupt universal forces and the lives of others on Earth. Our own bodies, which require peace, calmness, and harmony, can be tormented by these negative thoughts.

On one occasion, I called a good colleague in Canada to catch up on our life journeys. During the course of the conversation he told me that he could not control his negative thoughts. His life was going in the right direction and he was on the spiritual path, but he was plagued by negative thoughts about his own relationship. He had a constant fear of losing his relationship with the girl he loved, even though the girl was totally devoted and in love with him only. At the same time, his physical brain and daily well-being were impaired as his thoughts drove him crazy day and night. Eventually, he was able to control his thoughts (and his health) with prayers and positive affirmations.

When I inquired among my other friends, each one of them admitted that they had negative thoughts about work, health, finances, relationships, and families. I found varying degrees of ability to control negative thinking with my friends. I also observed that each one of us reacts differently to life situations according to individual sensitivity and level of spiritual consciousness. Take, for example, responses to being at the receiving end of hurtful words: some could ignore the insults and move ahead with life, while others would continuously get bogged down by what was said to them or how they were treated in life.

In all cases, it holds true that it is unwise to dwell on negative thoughts because, when taken to an extreme, such a tendency can become addictive—and spiritually dangerous. For if we start to enjoy wallowing in negativity, we are moving toward the darker side and alienating ourselves from God. The first step to spiritual awareness is to turn away from negative thoughts and to move toward the positive aspects of our lives. Prayers are the medium through which we can dismiss negative thoughts and see the light. Praying on a regular basis builds a wall of positivity around our physical bodies and minds, so that negative temptations are repelled and we will not absorb negativity.

Life provides all of us with opportunities to embrace the good or to accept the bad. The path of goodness can be a tough, steep climb. Meanwhile the path of badness and negativity can often be an easy, fruitful, and enjoyable stroll through life—for which the soul pays in the end. We each must decide what pleases our own soul and not our physical mind. We must become judges that make wise choices as we take life in our own hands in order to lead it on the good and godly path.

Goodness that lies within us will always exist. No one can take away the spirit of goodness from our hearts and souls. It will always be there no matter how tough life is. We need to use it wisely.

Thoughts Connect Our Lives

How we think is very powerful and important. Such a simple and loving thought as *I have faith in God and nothing can go wrong in my life* carries high positive energy. *I have the spark of God residing in me and no harm can come to me* is yet another powerful thought to distance us from negativity. Other examples include: *I am positive. I love God. I pray for my friend to be healthy. I love all my children.* These are all powerful thoughts that turn to powerful affirmations when spoken with pure positivity. Each thought creates a feeling of love and compassion, generating emotions from the physical mind to the heart and to the soul. Each thought triggers a chain of events that creates a pleasant feeling if it is positive. But if the thought is negative, it reverberates as an unpleasant feeling for self, others, and the universe.

Once we have released our negative thoughts, we have affected our own karma; this will emanate into the universe and come back to us through another chain of events in the future—in this lifetime or in succeeding lives.

Flow of Energy—Positive Words
Words can convey profound meaning. They have the power to stir emotions in another person. One kind, loving, or compassionate word from another person can change our lives and can make us feel loved and wanted. One unkind, ruthless, or demotivating word from someone can make us feel unloved, unworthy, and useless. It can stir emotions in our deepest selves. It can bring joy and happiness or it can cause pain and suffering. Conscious use of words can forge a bond of everlasting friendship, love, commitment, and trust; unconscious use of words can create anger, resentment, aloofness, distance, loneliness, loss of friendship, and disintegration of personal relationships.

We can use language to create different energy levels when we speak to others. Each word represents a different meaning and creates a flow of energy that is transmitted by the person who speaks and received by the person who is being addressed. Sometimes we are in a calm state of mind—happy and relaxed—and at other times we are full of anger—intense, irritable, and anxious. In the latter case, we are most likely to blurt out whatever comes into our physical minds. We do not stop to analyze the impact of our words and the reactions they will generate in others.

When we speak with consciously inspiring, positive words, we produce a corresponding response from the listener. *You are awesome, brilliant, charming, efficient,* excellent, fantastic, friendly, honest, intelligent, loving, motivating, pleasant, supportive, terrific, wonderful... Such words are apt to provoke good feelings in the recipient and a reciprocal flow of positive energy. Among the most powerful words we can say to one another are: *I love you. I care for you. You are always in my thoughts and prayers.*

In contrast, we also use negative words that are hurtful and demotivating. It is not difficult to imagine the flow of negative energy provoked by such words as *You are annoying, clumsy, ignorant, imperfect, loser, mean, repulsive, revolting, stupid, worthless* . . . Among the most hurtful words that we should avoid are: *You are a mistake. You should know where you stand. You are totally dumb.*

Positive words spark feelings of kindness, compassion, love, unity, friendship, peace, and togetherness for ourselves, others, and the universe. Negative words generate feelings of anger, hatred, and vengeance, thus inviting fights and arguments. Each word triggers a mechanism in other people, prompting them to react positively or negatively to us and to life. On the one hand, our words have the power to create love, liking, and respect; or on the other hand, indifference, dislike, and contempt. Often we are apt to utter negative words with greatest haste because we lack control of our physical minds and want only to be proved right or justified. When we have few strategies for communicating thoughts, we may resort to using mean and stupid words that hurt others and discourage them from speaking freely.

Harsh words delivered with an intent to hurt cannot be taken back. Once we use words to release negative energy, we create a blank space in our own environment and our physical body. We can then choose to fill up that space with something positive. If we are pure and connected with our higher selves, we will realize that our mean and spiteful words were damaging and feel compelled to apologize. Conveying apology and seeking forgiveness stem from a place of love and thus generate positive energy, not only for ourselves but also for the person who was hurt.

Although we expect life to treat us fairly in all respects, we often forget when it is our turn to treat others with respect, love, kindness, sympathy, and understanding. This is because we live in a materialistic world and at times would rather achieve something without regard for how it could hurt other people's feelings. But is this really the best way to act? Will it fulfill the true purpose of being alive? In our hearts, we know the answers to these questions.

If we know the answer, why don't we restrain ourselves from speaking harshly and negatively to others?

Flow of Energy—Positive Deeds

Our actions arise from our needs in life. Each action represents a selfish or a selfless interest. And the energy that we generate when we are selfish or selfless defines our character as individuals.

At times, our actions are manipulative and politically driven so that other people will behave in a way that helps us achieve a desired outcome for ourselves. We are not genuine when we act in this manner. Worst of all, to act in manipulative, selfish, self-centered, and ego-driven ways is to create and unleash negative energy.

What is the distinction between a person who is selfless and one who is selfish? A selfless person looks to the interest of other people. He or she puts any personal agenda aside and focuses on achieving a goal that will benefit another person. The selfless individual is not on an ego trip to gain career advancement or success at the expense of another human being. A selfish person is only interested in his or her own personal agenda, career, and advancement. Such a person wants to achieve personal goals and be number one in life at any cost and at the expense of other peoples' well-being.

Can we train ourselves to be selfless? Is it possible to learn the necessary traits from other human beings? The answer to both questions is yes.

Some souls are born selfless. This is often noticeable in families that have two or more children. We might find that one child is absolutely selfless and willing to share food and toys, whereas the other wants to keep everything. When souls are born on Earth, they bring with them the positive and negative soul characteristics that they have developed in their previous lives. If we are born with selfless characteristics, it is easier for us to lead a selfless life.

In other cases, upbringing and the environment at home or work changes us spiritually, enabling us to lead our lives in a new way. If we see our own parents, friends, peers, and colleagues behaving in a selfless manner, performing acts of service, we feel inspired and want to become role models like them. Such role models can potentially be found anywhere—in a family environment, schools, workplaces, or wherever else people come together and interact. Role models might be parents or grandparents, siblings, friends, teachers, fellow students, colleagues, bosses, community leaders, or spiritual advisors.

In my life, my grandfather was the inspiring figure who actually walked the talk of helping each and every person who came to him for assistance. Another memory that has stayed deep in my heart goes back to when I was a teenager and staying in a hostel in Mumbai. We would get our lunch and dinner from a catering company that was located nearby. To order food, we had to indicate in the register by a certain time each day whether we wanted lunch and dinner. One day early in my stay, I missed the opportunity to mark myself down for dinner. I only realized my mistake when I turned up for the meal. I was about to leave and return hungry to my room when the other boys told me not to worry and to join them for dinner. They assured me that my oversight happened all the time and that they always added one or two plates extra in case someone forgot to sign the register. I never forgot this experience. I was so inspired by the boys' gesture that it taught me at a young age to be selfless in my earthly journey.

As in my case, an everyday act of kindness can have life-changing consequences. The crucial enlightening experience might occur when a person is going through a difficult phase in life. It can touch us at any age—teens, twenties, thirties, forties, and so on. A person, known or unknown, lends a helping hand during a bad time. That particular help, no matter whether big or small, makes a lasting impact. The recipient's life changes for the better and he or she starts to look at the world from a different perspective. In this way compassion develops and spreads.

When others' selfless acts help us in our times of need, this makes a difference in our lives and we, too, want to be the instruments to help others change their lives. At such times we accept that we are part of God's plan and that what we went through had a deeper meaning than what we initially understood. Our perceptions change and we are transformed at a soul level. We are charged up and ready to serve others in any capacity, whether we are at work, at home with family, or even among strangers. Someone else's inspiration in life has become our own.

The opportunity to serve comes in different ways and at different stages of our lives. The opportunity will only come if we have both the ability and a genuine desire to help others on Earth. The universe does not expect us to give what we don't have. It expects us to give love, peace, hope, kindness, friendship, compassion, cooperation, unity, powerful and positive thoughts, positive words, and good deeds—all of which are essential for evolving the individual soul, spirit, and consciousness. We don't need to search far for ways to help others. Opportunities will present themselves when we are ready spiritually and willing to serve others with grace and humility. If we have a true desire to help someone, the doors of the universe will open for us, revealing those in need of our help and guidance.

Do not hesitate to help someone in life, because the moment you pause, the universe takes away the opportunity and offers it to another person. Meanwhile, you have missed a golden opportunity in life. There will be times when we will be at a crossroads, facing a tough choice about whether or not to offer help to someone. If, for example, you are unemployed and, outside a grocery store, you notice a man asking for money to buy lunch. When you consider the matter from your higher mind, you decide to help. After all, you have money to buy groceries, while he has no money for lunch. You are worried about tomorrow, while he is hungry today. Your soul consciousness tells you what to do.

A kind act is never forgotten and kindness will be ingrained at a soul level. I have learnt from my life experience that when someone has helped me, the universe connects me to another person, often years later, who is seeking similar assistance. When you are faced with such a situation, your higher mind recalls the help you once received and, without a second thought, you now extend your own helping hand. The power and energy of the universe is always revolving. Today, when you need help, you receive help. Tomorrow, someone else will need help and, to the extent of your power, you will provide it without hesitation.

We all go through spiritual learning experiences in our lives and these create permanent impressions in our minds. The greatest lesson is to strive for selflessness, to dedicate our energies to serving others. What is the sense of being born on Earth and achieving all the good things life, if we remain reluctant to sacrifice even a tiny bit of our time and energy to put a smile on someone else's face? The more sacrificing and giving we become in life, the greater will be the spiritual growth of our souls.

As individuals, we may have soul characteristics embedded in us from our previous life or we may possess other traits that predispose us to selflessness. To be truly selfless, a person's inner desire to serve others should be far greater than any ambition to succeed in earthly life. When the ideal of service dominates personal goals, we tend to see the world and our lives from a broad perspective. We feel focused, drawn to others, connected to the universe, and spiritually aligned. Our lives, in other words, have purpose and we are living to our fullest potential on Earth. We thus have inner peace and a sense of accomplishment that we could never feel even if we had completed the toughest project in the workplace and earned a huge promotion.

To my mind, the essence of selflessness is the willingness to look beyond our own happiness to create happiness for someone else. As souls and human beings, we need to devote our time to listening to others in life. Our friends, family, children, spouses, and coworkers will only be drawn to us if we have the listening skills and are not shutting them off by not listening to them. Our role on Earth provides us the platform on which to serve, whether on a business, personal, or soul level. When we connect with colleagues, we have achieved a meaningful business or professional goal. When we connect on a personal level, we have strengthened our bonds with friends and family. And when we connect on a soul level, we have served someone else—and arrived at a new destination in life.

Among our duties as souls is the imperative to guide others along the path of consciousness. In other words, this means helping them take the right spiritual action on Earth. When someone comes to us for advice, we are teacher, guide, and mentor. We should be willing to listen and provide the spiritual advice that we judge to be in the person's best interest. We should not be focused on our own power, prestige, or image. The true advisory role is to unselfishly provide guidance from the higher mind, to help illuminate the path of greater consciousness, and to allow latitude for others to make the right choices. Ultimately, we all have free will to make our own decisions. Thus we, ourselves, plot the course of our own spiritual journeys on Earth and shape our own destinies.

Becoming Selfless

Let us now take the opportunity to explore some of the characteristics that promote selflessness in our personal and working lives. Is there a magic formula that will distinguish one person from another? No, there is no single perfect combination of selfless traits, but certain qualities of mind and heart nurture the growth of selflessness. Among the important characteristics that I feel lead to selflessness are compassion, humility, kindness, and sincerity. Some individuals might possess these characteristics in various degrees, while others might lack certain of them. There is no right or wrong formula, as your specifically selfless traits depend on your overall level of consciousness.

Acts of selflessness are appreciated by many but not accepted by all. People who have the habit of putting themselves first instead of serving others might find a selfless act threatening to their own egos, power, or positions. Such people are unaccustomed, or even hostile, to behaviors that do not require external validation by others. Selflessness, in contrast, is pure; it springs from soul consciousness and is an inspiration to others. A selfless act by one person creates a ripple effect—as it emanates outward to touch countless lives.

Selflessness emerges from a combination of our personal traits and spiritual learning experiences in life. It never develops overnight. But can we consciously shift our personalities to foster our own growth toward selflessness? Happily, the answer is yes. So, how do we make that shift?

I realized that we cannot move toward selflessness if we are always, angry, irritated, and impatient. The shift happens when we are calm, willing to let go of our egos, and open to trusting our higher selves to make conscious choices. The words of Lao Tzu (604 BC–531 BC), a poet and philosopher of ancient China, are as true today as ever:

> Watch your thoughts; they become words. Watch your words; they become actions. Watch your actions; they become habit. Watch your habits; they become character. Watch your character; it becomes your destiny.

Selflessness thus develops in stages as we learn to sacrifice our own happiness for the benefit of others. Our progress may not always be steady and at times we may falter. When we are tempted to think, speak and act negatively, we need to ask ourselves these questions:

1. Will this thought, words and action serve any purpose in my life?
2. Is this thought, words and action harmful to me and my spirit?
3. Is this thought, words and action going to bring happiness to me, the person(s) directly involved, immediate friends and family, and anyone else?
4. How would I react if someone in this universe were to think, speak and act similarly toward me?
5. Will this thought, words and action bring me inner peace, joy, and happiness?

The answers to the above questions will serve as a guide in leading a meaningful life on earth.

Selfless Acts Generate Positive Energy
A selfless act always generates positive energy for both the person who performs the act and the person who is being helped. This energy is the highest energy that we can give others in life. Selfless acts can stir up positive emotions and inspire others to take the lead and be more giving in life. Such acts link one soul's positive energy to another soul's energy and the energy generated from this act leaves a hidden spark in the heart of the person who received the selfless gift. The spark never diminishes—it glows at a high frequency, illuminating the question that is at the core of spiritual growth: How do I turn my life around to help other human beings on Earth?

Rabindranath Tagore (1861–1942), Indian philosopher, poet, and winner of the Nobel Prize for literature in 1913, said, "I slept and dreamt that life was joy. I awoke and saw that life was service. I acted and, behold, service was joy." The more we help others selflessly, the more we will want to help. The more we want to help, the wider the doors of the universe will open up to us to render help. And the more we render help, the more we deliver prosperity to the universe. What is most important to remember is that when we help others, we shine light into the universe that will never be lost but will always glow in the hearts of all those who have received our help and grace.

• • •

Inspirational Connections

- You constantly produce energy via thought, word, and deed; your energy is either positive or negative.
- Soul development and energy are interconnected—the higher your soul's consciousness, the more positive its energy, and vice versa.
- You become what you think, say, and do—you have the power, or free will, to shape your destiny by controlling your thoughts, words, and deeds.
- Selflessness—serving others—is the way of spiritual growth.
- Your duty as a soul is to progress toward selflessness and to help others along the same path.
- A kind act is never forgotten and kindness is ingrained at a soul level.
- Your happiness comes from the happiness of others.

3
Managing Positive and Negative Energies

*People deal too much with the negative,
with what is wrong. Why not try and
see positive things, to just touch those
things and make them bloom?*

—ThichNhat Hanh

OUR SOULS ARE only interested in positive thoughts, words, and deeds, but our physical minds and egos draw us toward negative influences in life. Each person possesses a combination of positive and negative energies. Some might possess more positive energy and less negative, while others might have more negative and less positive. The energy that resides in us determines the level of our consciousness and is the driving force in the individual's journey on Earth. People who have strong positive energy will be able to control the negative energy that resides in them and surrounds them.

Negative energy cannot affect us unless we let it. This is simple in theory, but dealing with negative energy in reality can be more complicated. For, all too often, our own energies can clash with those of another individual. This happens when we are on a higher frequency (positive energy) and are surrounded by others on a lower frequency (negative energy). In such instances, our energies do not flow in harmony. Our higher selves feel uncomfortable and we want to move away from the person, situation, and environment. If we do not distance ourselves from the negative energy, those who are generating it can drain us of our own positive energy.

If, however, our own stores of positive energy are abundant, we are less likely to be affected by the negativity and may even be able to bring about some change in the other person through our positive energy and presence. Our positive thoughts can inspire others to make the spiritual switch in their lives on Earth. It is up to us how we use our infinite energies. When we use them for good, we constantly replenish our positive energy—while espousing negativity depletes the energy that drives all our finest emotions in life. When we start using negative energy, we isolate ourselves from feelings of love, kindness, compassion, grace, humility, and faith. We should not, therefore, encourage the negative but focus instead on the positive. Positivity is the path to higher consciousness, the light that outshines negativity.

If we have a sincere desire to change our lives, we as individuals need to be positive, act in positive ways, and generate feelings of positivity all around us. If everyone were to have at least one positive thought every hour, magnify the effect and impact on Earth and imagine the impact on our environment and our lives. Positivity can transform us, others, nature, and the universe. We need to use our time and power on Earth to champion positivity and thus to enrich our own and others' lives. Change is difficult but, with one step in the right direction, everything is possible. We are all connected, and we all have the responsibility to generate a positive and loving environment for our own selves and others. Whatever we do, and however we live and lead others, let us not forget that our ultimate purpose in life is to build a better world and a better future.

Although most of us believe in this ideal, there are situations in which we can all too easily lose sight of it. This happens when we find ourselves in circumstances where disparate personalities come together, where pressures are often high and disagreements inevitable. Nowhere are such conditions more common and apparent than in the workplace. Since most of us must spend a great part of our time earning a living, it is important that we consider how energies can clash at work.

Positive and Negative Energies in the Work Environment

Have you ever found that you feel drained when you are near some people? Or have you noticed that certain individuals always make others uncomfortable? This is all related to our energy, and the consequences in the workplace can be both personal and collective.

Departmental meetings are a commonplace in many working environments. Their effectiveness and how individuals experience them are in large part a matter of energy. I recall an instance in which Tracy, VP of Financial Services, had called a meeting with the Finance team. Pauline, the Finance Manager, was one of the attendees. Tracy had just come from another meeting and sat next to her.

Pauline's day was going well and she was in high spirits. Tracy was irritable, brimming with anger and other negative emotions, because things were not going her way. The moment Tracy sat next to her, Pauline felt her energy draining out. She felt uncomfortable and depleted, and did not even have the will to reason in the meeting. When it was over and she returned to her own work station, she had no energy for anything but reading her emails and wished the day would end. She made the wise choice of leaving the office early.

At home, in a different environment, she noticed her energies recharging slowly. She went to sleep early and the next day awoke reenergized. There was nothing wrong with her physical body. Unable to manage the negative energy surrounding her, Pauline's soul needed precious time in a different atmosphere. Her positive energy had been challenged by Tracy's negativity.

The example of Pauline and Tracy illustrates how one person's energy can affect another's. An individual's energy can also have a much wider impact. It can affect team or other group energy, which then impacts the department and even the larger corporate environment. In an organizational setting, each person is therefore responsible for generating positive energy. An employee that is always positive and advocating for positivity is on a higher frequency than many others. This counteracts the effects created by coworkers on lower frequencies.

Let us take a simple example of a team of twenty employees. If there were nine individuals operating on low frequency and always negative—speaking ill of others and not being positive about the work and environment—this creates a negative energy in the department as a whole, unless the positive energy of the other team members is greater than the combined negativity of the nine members. The trouble is that the energy imbalance, although favouring the positive, nonetheless causes the team to function less effectively than it could. The moment that there is a change and all team members start thinking positively, it shows in the improved results.

Let's for a moment assume that all nine negative employees had to attend a training session in another location and the department is only full of positive team members. These members are creating a feeling of unity, friendship, and bonding with one another. Imagine the new feeling, the higher frequency, and the lightness in the environment. If you are on a positive frequency, you will be drawn toward this energy because it is the same energy that you as an individual possess and find most comfortable. Negative team members attract other negative team members. They are unable to draw positive team members onto their side, because that is not how energies work.

Whenever I think of energy and how it impacts a team, I recall Rachel, who was a manager in a large organization—and full of negative energy. She was always complaining about too much work and not enough productivity within the team. She micromanaged, controlling each team member's every action. She was picky and convinced that she was always right; she could not work with the weaknesses of another team member. She was always finding fault and, to justify her own shortcomings, would cast blame onto her team's performance. She was never satisfied with the work, the team or the environment.

Rachel's self-centredness—no doubt overcompensation for low self-esteem—was generating exceptionally negative energy. And this was being absorbed by the whole team. People in the department were like zombies, working long hours to produce work but without any sense of fulfillment. They saw little purpose in coming to work. Their individuality and creativity were compromised and they had no reason to perform at their best. They felt worthless and useless, since Rachel was perpetually targeting their weaknesses. What little energy they brought to work each day was soon depleted. When they went home, demoralized, they brought negative energy with them that impacted their spouses and children.

If you were Rachel, how would you want your employees to remember you in life? How do you want them to think about you after work? What kinds of comments are the employees making about you? The whole cycle is negative, negative, and negative. It is truly dispiriting. In this situation, the circle of negativity will never end unless Rachel is transferred to another place or department or, alternatively, the team members find a way to work around her behaviour in a positive way. Positivity in such a situation is indeed challenging and no one could be faulted for hoping that Rachel is replaced by another manager with a more productive attitude.

My experience has been that a person who is manipulative, lacking in empathy and integrity, and unable or unwilling to speak the truth will not create positive energy and will not work well with colleagues who are transparent, truthful, honest, and collaborative. These two kinds of people will never be in harmony since they are not on the same energy frequency—the disconnect is at a soul level. Such situations will never be easy, but we can make them as workable as possible. As leaders, employees, and human beings, we have an obligation to control our own spiritual weaknesses; we do so by consciously and consistently striving to generate positive energy.

Energies create connection among souls. The more we radiate positive energy, the stronger the bond we create with employees and teams. Energies can transform teams and the combined positive energies of teams and the leader can transform the productivity of the work. The energy that we create as a manager or an employee also bounces back to us in the same fashion. It is the law of nature. We cannot change unless we shift our consciousness by being ethical, moral, professional, and positive in our thoughts, words, and actions.

Negative Feelings and Forgiveness
I have observed from early childhood that negative thoughts are the crux of our problems. We need to empty our minds of anger, vengefulness, and un-forgivingness and replace these with more loving and positive thoughts. If we are seeking true happiness, we need to forget the past and move ahead into a more comfortable place where peace and love prevail. Only when we discard negative thoughts and feelings will we unburden ourselves and lighten our souls. Negative feelings draw us down in energy, eroding

our spirits, creating imbalance in our physical minds, and distorting our view of the world. We see only negative all around us and cannot perceive God's grace, kindness, and humility.

Our negative feelings can create self-pity in us, which may somewhat satisfy our physical minds but does not work for our souls. The soul wants to move beyond self-pity. When we indulge in self-pity, our understanding is distorted. We are failing to grasp God's plan for our souls to develop spiritually. It is important to grasp that the things that upset us most can show us the path to improving our souls. What brings us grief can also awaken our souls, help us evolve, and bring us closer to God.

The way forward is to accept what life offers us on Earth. We must remember the experience but forget the hurt that people have inflicted on us—forget these people and forgive them. When we forgive, we move ahead in life and feel lighter in mind, heart, and spirit. We can see the bigger picture and the meaning of our own journey on Earth. Forgiveness elevates the soul and is the crucial step to end the cycle of a particular karma.

Every incident, good or bad, pleasant or unpleasant, has a deeper meaning for each soul. What one soul learns differs from what another person will grasp from the same event. But the particular lessons that we learn have the same larger goals: to evolve and improve our souls; to make meaningful changes in the lives of ourselves and others; and to draw nearer to God. For God wants us all to be closer to his spirit and to travel the path of righteousness, selflessness, kindness, and grace. We need to accept this, our shared journey, and step forward with a smile, not backward to the past. There is no sense in holding on to the grudges of the past when we have a beautiful future ahead of us. We must move ahead full faith and confidence—move with positivity and gratitude for all the blessings we have received in life for ourselves and for our families.

Learning forgiveness never ends. It makes us wise and pure. It makes us understand the meaning of our lives and our choices. Such learning helps us evolve our souls and serve others. It stays embedded in our souls when we pass on to the spirit world, and we bring back the wisdom when we are reborn on Earth.

Energies and the World around Us
The energies that we generate from day to day not only impact us but also affect our surroundings—whether home, workplace, or the greater environment in which we all live and breathe. We each have a social responsibility toward the various environments that we personally inhabit, and we must further contribute to protecting Earth for all mankind and future generations. Our thoughts, words, and actions impact us, our family, friends, co-workers, homes, and workplaces. The collective energy that we emanate as a society impacts the overall environment and surrounds us with the same energy that we helped generate in the first place.

Ensuring that positive energy pervades all our environments starts with our own contribution. What can we do as individuals to generate positive thoughts, words, and actions? What will be our contribution for the day is important. It matters how polite and kind we are to our fellow human beings on Earth and to our employees and colleagues.

Using our earthly power positively and providing selfless service contribute to keeping all our environments—including nature itself—pure and clean. Why are people constantly longing to take a vacation in another country, place, or city? Why do people need more vacation time every year? People take vacations to enjoy and relax in new environments. But it is also possible that holidays are necessary for some people because they have contaminated their own environments at work and at home. When they enter a new environment, they feel at peace because the energy level is different and positive. While taking a vacation is good for the soul, it is nonetheless crucial to maintain calmness and positivity at home and work. That way, a holiday is a matter of choice.

Changing Our Consciousness
If we have positive energy, we will always want to be an instrument to create peace, love, harmony, and contentment—in ourselves, others, and the world around us. If we have negative energy, we will only be comfortable where there is discord and disharmony. Life creates opportunities for our souls to grow spiritually, but we do not always take advantage of these opportunities. At times, when our ego dictates the terms by which we live, we can harbour hatred, jealousy, and the craving for revenge.

When the ego, along with its negativity, takes over, we need to bring it under control and operate from the higher self. We do this by changing our negative thoughts, words, and actions to positive thoughts, words, and actions. Any thought, word, or deed that brings pain and misery to others should be avoided at all cost. Any thought, word, or deed that promotes peace, love, joy, and happiness originates from pure consciousness and is the ideal to which to aspire. As we strive for ever-greater positivity, we undergo a transformation that enables us to

1. See a difference in our own lives;
2. Find peace, love, and connection with others;
3. Experience light and kindness flowing through our minds, bodies, and spirits; and
4. Feel completeness of spirit and soul.

The more positive energy that we generate, the calmer and more open we are to life's infinite possibilities. In addition to thinking, speaking, and acting positively, we can further produce positive energy through prayer and the stillness of meditation. In all such instances, we are consciously choosing to be positive and to operate from our higher selves. In this way we elevate the consciousness of our souls, create our own journeys on Earth, and shape the kind of future we desire.

Divine Energy

What is divine energy? Divine energy is a source of power that we all possess as souls but are either afraid to tap or ignorant of the fact that such an energy exists within us. Divine energy is generated at a soul level and is constantly connected to our consciousness.

We might be physically fit and strong but spiritually weak and dim; divine energy might exist but flicker as a low flame. Souls who are on the spiritual path and have developed to a certain level possess a totally different divine energy. It is brightly illuminated, steady, and radiant with qualities of healing and nurturing. This divine energy has only one purpose: to serve the Master of the divine energy who in turn will serve other souls on Earth.

Divine energy not only radiates brightness, strength, and positivity, but it also spreads in all directions. The person possessing strong divine energy might touch or heal a person physically and emotionally. This ignites pure joy in the person who is the recipient of divine energy. Such energy is so powerful that it only breeds positivity and eradicates negativity.

Divine energy vibrates with different colours and, depending on the frequency of the individual, surrounds the person with a particular colour; this is how some souls project their divine energy. In some souls, divine energy is manifested as intuition, a talent for guiding others, healing powers, or the ability to make wise choices in life. In whatever form it takes, divine energy has only one purpose: to promote peace, joy, harmony, and love in the universe.

Divine energy can be blocked in certain individuals because they are not authentic in how they live. They do not portray a genuine image of themselves and are not true to their own selves. Divine energy can only spark within us when we are able to love our true selves and other human beings. Divine energy illuminates at the level of our consciousness. If our consciousness is elevated and connected to the higher self, divine energy will illuminate brightly within us and shine all around us. It will create an intense feeling of peace and joy within us that extends to all other souls with whom we connect on a daily basis.

If we all believed that divine energy is linked to our consciousness and that the soul is immortal, the effect on individual actions would be immense. We would all start to behave decently to all human beings on Earth. We would stop hurting our fellow human beings in all respects and would always strive to be selfless, loving, and nurturing in all our relationships. And we would do so in the clear knowledge that our actions were furthering our spiritual progress and the advancement of our souls.

Channelling Our Energies

Energy is generated best when we become as concerned about others as we are about ourselves—when we wish for others what we wish for ourselves, dream for others as we dream for ourselves, pray for others as we pray for our own selves and loved ones, and do exactly the same for others as we do for family and ourselves. When we follow these standards, we are truly looking at each and every person as equal to ourselves. We are accepting each and every person as a creation of God and we are loving others with the same energy that we bestow on ourselves and those closest to us.

Please do not wait for someone to show you the path of love. We can blend love into any relationship whether it is with our parents, spouses, siblings, friends, children, bosses, or co-workers. If love is the channel through which to build healthy relationships and strong bonds of friendship, why do we not use it? The reasons are various: We fear that being loving might be viewed as being weak or cowardly. We are afraid that someone will reject us and our love. We even worry that we will be laughed at. What is more important to focus on is this: when we are blending love into any relationship, we are using the energy of

God that resides in us. The quicker we accept this principle, the easier it becomes for us to be loving toward our fellow human beings.

When we think positively, we are channelling our energy to change ourselves for the better. When we use the same positive energy to think well of others, we bring the same favourable results to them. Negativity is a temptation that alienates us from our true selves, our higher minds, and most of all, from God. When we use negativity in any situation, we do not please our true selves, our higher minds, or God. All we please is our own self-image—our ego. We please the ego at the cost of degrading the spirit and soul in order to justify selfish actions and pride. We serve the illusion but not the reality. We serve the darkness and negativity but not the light and love of God.

Thoughts are the channels for manifesting our destiny, for changing it from good to bad and vice versa. Each thought, word, and deed is linked and interwoven into a karmic pattern. The moment we think, speak, or act negatively, we build negative karma. The moment we think, speak, or act positively, we bring the grace of God into our lives.

• • •

Inspirational Connections

- The more positive energy you have, the more you can control the negative energy in and around you.
- Negative energy impacts you, those with whom you interact, and the world around you—including home, the workplace, and the natural environment.
- Forgiveness dissipates negative energy, elevates the soul, and brings you closer to God.
- Using positive energy to promote forgiveness, peace, love, harmony, and contentment raises your consciousness.
- Divine energy is the highest form of positive energy; whether dormant or burning brightly, it resides within you.
- By channelling your energies through love and positivity, you will improve your karma and grow closer to God.

4
Karma—
the Universal Law

Things don't just happen in this world of arising and passing away. We don't live in some kind of crazy, accidental universe. Things happen according to certain laws, laws of nature. Laws such as the law of karma, which teaches us that as a certain seed gets planted, so will that fruit be.

—*Sharon Salzberg*

WHEN I WAS YOUNG, I had a misconception about karma. I thought that if I did something wrong to someone, someone would do the same negative thing to me in my current life. How wrong I was and how distorted was my thinking in the early stages of my life. Later I came to know correctly that karma is the law of spiritual learning. It is the law that monitors our actions, good and bad, keeping a log in our higher minds. It helps us understand and benefit from the lessons in spirituality that life teaches us. It helps us refine our souls. The universe is governed by the principle of cause and effect. What we do to others will be returned to us; and how we think, speak, and act has a cyclic effect in our lives and in the universe. If we think negatively, speak negatively, and act negatively, we are adding negative karma to our own lives. If our thoughts are angry, destructive, hateful, jealous, lustful, or vengeful, we are creating karma accordingly. If we speak hurtful and mean-spirited words or if our actions are bullying, cruel, condemning, controlling, deceiving, manipulative, revengeful, egoistical, heartless, or humiliating, we are adding negative karma to our lives. If, on the other hand, we are kind, compassionate, loving, humble, forgiving, and selfless, we are creating good karma.

We are each subject to the working of karma. We cannot escape or hide from it. We cannot manipulate ourselves or our lives in order to bypass or deceive karma. Karma is the sum total of our choices and actions in our current life, and past life choices and actions. If we repay our individual karma silently without any grumbling, this eases our way through life and we do not build additional negative karma.

Karma and the Flow of Life

Life is a river. We have to flow with our lives, with whatever comes our way. Life is a challenge. One fine day we have everything, and the next day we might not have anything. One day we are in the perfect job, and the next day we might be struggling to find employment. One day we have perfect relationships with our loved ones and the next day we might find our relationships broken, our loved ones lost to us due to death or stupid misunderstandings. Life opens doors and shuts others in our faces.

Life also brings us opportunities to help others and to receive help in return. The flow of life demonstrates that love is the ultimate experience in all relationships—when we love, we can overcome our weaknesses and overlook the shortcomings of others. Life teaches us humility, patience, and positivity. Life is a gift from God and can strengthen our soul connection to God. How we each live life is a matter of individual choice. Ideally, we will each use the gift of life wisely for the betterment of our souls by helping others. Each of our lives on Earth is special and each of us has the mission to lead our lives with honesty, integrity and peace. The more that we elect to do so, the better will be our individual karma.

The Universality of Karma
The law of karma is both universal and uniform. It operates the same way for all of us, whether we are rich or poor, famous or obscure, of high status or low. Karma is not partial to any individual, country, or environment. Attached to each soul, it is inescapable and follows us even if we migrate to another country. Karma is a continuous process that spans many individual lifetimes. We therefore carry our karma with us when we die, and we bring it back upon rebirth. As the all-encompassing law of spiritual learning, karma is fair to all souls. It is never partial to anyone and is embedded in our souls whether we like it or not, and whether we believe in it or not.

The law of karma was created to help all souls become one with the Creator and assist the Creator's divine plan. The law of karma helps each soul learn to diminish negative characteristics by seeking to perfect such God-created virtues as kindness, compassion, forgiveness, and humility. Each soul was born to glow and not to deteriorate in spirit. Only when we embrace these virtues, do we rise spiritually and become able to see the divine essence through the eyes of our souls. Karma for each soul is to find perfection in each and every soul attribute. When the perfection is attained, the soul moves on to the next level of consciousness.

Building Bad—and Good—Karma

Karma is built by our own doing and we are thus the masters of our own destinies. The more we give into temptations and negativity, the more we create bad karma. The more we resist negativity, making right and pious choices, the more we eventually build good karma, which in turn converts into grace from God.

Our role on Earth is to think about each and every act before we do it. If our thinking is distorted, eventually everything will go wrong. The images that we create in our minds correspond to realities in the universe. The wisdom is to distinguish and cultivate the images from the higher mind and to weed out the images of lower consciousness that hinder us from seeing the universe as perfect, loving, and exquisite. The essence of karma is to learn to love others unconditionally and thus to ensure that all our actions are loving, positive, and peaceful. The greatest peace is not achieved through fights and wars. It is achieved through love and the understanding that we each need to take the first step in generating peace and love. It is crucial to forgive those who have caused pain and suffering in our lives, for once we do so, we have learned a spiritual lesson and ended that particular karma.

Some people might be inclined to think of karma in the following way: *For the past ten years, I have not harmed, deceived, cheated, or insulted anyone in my life. I am following God's path. So why do I still keep encountering difficult challenges in life?* The answer lies in the fact that karma works over a long period of time. Ten years of following God's path may not be sufficient to counteract your bad karma, which may have been built in both this life and previous lives. Soul evolvement is a gradual, continuous process.

There are times when a soul decides to take rebirth just to pay off a specific negative karma. There are souls who have done tremendous harm to others in their previous lives; their spirits are totally misaligned and distorted. They, themselves, may choose to be born as special-needs people, because it is only when they go through this kind of life on Earth that they are able to pay off the karma they have accumulated. The soul who decides to take birth in this particular fashion chooses the mother and the family who will help him or her with this tough journey on Earth.

Parents who are blessed with such a child, may think, God, why me? What did I do to deserve this? There are various possible answers and no single correct one. It could be, for example, that you as a parent need to learn calmness and patience. Or perhaps you require a lesson in self-sacrifice. In any case, you were born to serve someone in this fashion to improve your soul consciousness. Sometimes one of the siblings becomes particularly attached to the special child and they become inseparable as souls on Earth. They share love, soul connection, and a flow of energy that is invisible to the eye. The flow of energy is mutual love generating at the level of soul consciousness, and such love can bring unity and peace to the whole family.

Knowing the significance of karma, and how it operates, we each need to assess how we lead our daily lives. Are we pure in our thoughts, words, and actions? For the law of karma dictates that when we are thinking, speaking, and acting negatively toward others, we are building negative karma for our own selves; and when the other person thinks, speaks, and acts negatively toward us and we do not react, the other person builds his own unfavourable karma.

Many people talk mainly about the negative effects of karma. But we also need to remember that we build good karma through selfless acts, kind words, positive thoughts and affirmations, assisting others in times of need, listening to others, providing correct guidance and advice, helping others to understand the spiritual laws, and showing them the spiritual path to lead and live by. Good karma may come to each of us in the form of a healthy life, blessed family and children, loyal friends, and a loving spouse who is also a spiritual partner. We cannot see the effects of good karma because it is not tangible or visible. Good karma is a blessing, protection, and grace from God. Life is sometimes so tough that the good karma we have banked is necessary to help us go through our tough tests and training on Earth.

Two Lawyers—Two Kinds of Karma

The stories of two men, both lawyers, illustrates how karma works according to the individual choices that we make when we come face-to-face with life's tests:

Mark was born into a good family and had a comfortable living. He graduated with a law degree and started his practice in India. He started with good intentions of helping people with all their legal needs, and people came to trust him. He developed more clients because of his honesty and integrity. All was going well in his life till one day his uncle, who was in his eighties, sought his guidance about drafting a will and transferring all of his property to his family. As Mark analyzed his uncle's property documents, he became increasingly upset as greed assaulted his mind. To his surprise, he learned that his uncle owned many properties, some of them in prime locations, and they were worth millions of dollars. Mark wondered whether any other relatives were aware of this fortune.

In a meeting with his uncle a week later, they went over the draft documents for the will, power of attorney, and property transfers. The uncle requested some minor changes and Mark assured him that all these would be done. Meanwhile, Mark's mind was still playing a tug of war between finalizing the documents as requested or letting greed take control and transferring the property to his younger brother's name. When he called his brother and revealed his plan, the brother was excited and agreed to play along. Mark accordingly substituted his brother's name for the uncle's nephew in the documents. Having faith in Mark, the uncle signed the legal papers without bothering to read them.

Life then took a different turn for Mark and his brother. A few months passed and the uncle died peacefully in his sleep. Mark and his brother sold the prime real estate property at a peak price and invested the proceeds heavily in shares and other real estate properties. They wanted to make money faster than it could be printed by the Reserve Bank of India. Although they enjoyed success with whatever they bought, they never felt content in their hearts. They became ever greedier and started swindling clients who had no family or dependants. At the same time, to show others that they were good citizens and pillars of society, they supported charities and opened foundations to help the needy.

Ultimately, none of their deceptions worked. In 1992, the Bombay Stock Exchange took a heavy dive, and all the shares that Mark and his brother were holding lost their worth. With the stock market crashing, the real estate market fell and the brothers also lost the money they had invested in the real estate. Although they had enjoyed their ill-gotten wealth for a short period of time, they lost it all and built negative karma.

In the same city there was another lawyer, named Roy, who came from a family that included many lawyers. Since he grew up in a household where law was discussed all the time, he, too, graduated with a law degree. When he was in university, he started putting in a few hours each day with his dad and his uncle at the office. He wanted to learn and had a passion to help others in life. The more he worked with his dad, the more challenging he found it to work with the law. His dad would make him sit in meetings to listen to complex problems faced by clients in day-to-day life. After a meeting was over, Roy would discuss his point of view, and his dad would either correct his misunderstandings or congratulate him on his brilliant ideas. From his dad and uncle he learnt the importance of dealing ethically with clients, their money, and their property; most of all, he became committed to upholding trust, honesty, and integrity.

The business was performing well but not flourishing. Roy finished his law degree and joined his dad. He upheld the values of his family in performing his business, and he also started doing pro bono work for people who could not afford legal services. He assisted people of all ages and, most of all, enjoyed helping troubled youth and showing them the spiritual path. To him service was everything and seeing a positive change in someone was more gratifying than making money. In choosing to lead his life with caring and compassion for others, Roy demonstrated a soul-level awareness of karmic law—an understanding that, as human beings, our role in life is to improve spiritually and that the resultant good karma helps us through our tests and tough times on Earth.

Karma and Consciousness
The stories of Mark and Roy demonstrate the strong correlation between karma and soul consciousness. Roy made selfless choices from his higher mind; the more he served others, the more elevated became his spiritual consciousness and the more he added to his good karma. Mark, on the other hand, made his choices from a low level of consciousness; the results lowered his consciousness all the more and increased his karmic debt. Thus he denied his responsibility in life—the responsibility that is common to us all: to grow in spirituality and consciousness and to repay our individual karma.

For the soul to evolve—like Roy, and unlike Mark—we must rise above the misconceptions of our physical minds, learn life's spiritual lessons, and grow in consciousness by embracing positivity and right action in all spheres of our lives. The higher a soul's consciousness, the faster will be the repayment of his or her karma. For the higher the consciousness, the tougher are the tests and training on Earth, because the soul is evolved enough to undergo the rigorous challenges that further spiritual growth demands. At times, our previously accumulated good karma, or grace, may be available to help us repay our negative karma in stages, because our actions were so harmful in previous lives that our souls would not have the strength to endure the harsh tests necessary to learn all our spiritual lessons at once.

For many souls, repaying bad karma is a lengthy and often uneven endeavour. When the required effort feels most daunting to us, it is helpful to remember that the journey to higher consciousness is as important as the destination. And if our steps toward spiritual growth at times seem faltering, we can always take heart from the knowledge that we are nonetheless progressing along the right path. The universe is not accidental but designed, and the law of karma is not to hinder but to help us in our evolution toward the Divine. As we strive to tap into our higher minds, to become positive and conscious in everything we do, we are acting with pure intentions—and thus awakening the Spirit within us.

• • •

Inspirational Connections

- Karma is the law governing your spiritual learning.
- Negative thoughts, words, and deeds create karmic debt; karma is repaid by thinking, speaking, and acting with positivity, selflessness, and forgivingness.
- Life is a gift, and your earthly mission is to live it with honesty, integrity, and peace; to do so—or not—is a matter of your own choice.
- Karma is universal and fair to all souls.
- Consciousness and karma are interrelated; you are born on Earth to repay your karmic debt and to raise your spiritual consciousness.
- Karma is your soul's pathway to oneness with the Divine.

5
Spiritual Learning and Soul Development

Sometimes, reaching out and taking someone's hand is the beginning of a journey. At other times, it is allowing another to take yours.

—Vera Nazarian

HOW MANY TIMES have we heard parents wish for a better child? Or children ask for better parents? Similarly, employees want better bosses, and leaders would like better teams to manage. None of this is a coincidence. We are all connected at a soul level and were meant to be together to learn spiritual lessons from one another.

Spiritual learning is a continuous evolutionary process, and one of life's basic requirements. It never ends. We were all born on Earth to learn to reduce our negative soul characteristics, while also working to retain our positive soul traits. As souls before birth, that is what we promised to do in our earthly lives. But often, once we are born, we encounter challenges and difficulties that distract us from our original promise. We then fall into the trap of trying to rationalize with our physical minds in order to justify our wrongdoing. Instead of overcoming our negative soul characteristics, we either build more of them, or compromise our positive traits. Thus the individual increases his or her karmic debt and the soul regresses. When this happens, we are in a state of depleted consciousness and feel disconnected from God. This disconnection brings with it a sense of personal emptiness and unworthiness that will not go away till we raise our consciousness and start following the godly path by making conscious choices in life. In other words, we must persevere in learning our spiritual lessons.

Earthly versus Spiritual Learning
Earthly learning increases our knowledge but the greater lessons of the spirit make us wise and help evolve our souls. Earthly and spiritual forms of learning are intertwined. But this does not necessarily mean that the usual successes of our earthly journeys—career achievements, prosperity, and acclaim—reflect success in our spiritual journeys. Quite the opposite might be the case.

From the time that we are born, we begin to master the basics of earthly existence. We learn to talk, walk, and behave. We acquire certain formal skills so that we can practise a profession or trade, perhaps even fulfil our dreams and passions. We also develop and refresh our skills by attending seminars and workshops to expand our horizons, to sharpen our skills, and to develop as leaders in the workplace and community.

Spiritual learning is different—it does not come from acquiring formal skills but from interacting and coexisting with other human beings. Earth is the school for the soul and it is in this dimension that the soul learns to build positive characteristics of kindness, compassion, peace, forgivingness, and patience. The Earth school allows us to be connected with one another so that we can share our spiritual experience, overcome our weaknesses and fears, and contribute our gifts and talents for the benefit of other human beings. In this way, our spirits transform and our souls evolve. The trouble is, in our fast-paced environments, we tend to forget our main purpose for being born on Earth. We become too materialistic and selfish to such an extent that we want everything to ourselves; we forget about sharing, caring, kindness, compassion, and empathy. Many earthly environments teach us to achieve, even at the expense of others. In such scenarios, the ego is never satisfied and peace does not dominate our lives. All seems fair in the game of advancement, greed, competitiveness, and power. There is no moment of truth or silence to soothe the body, mind, heart, and spirit.

The more we try to search for peace, the less of it we find, for the simple reason that we are looking in the wrong direction. Instead of fulfilling our soul's promise to grow spiritually, we try to run at the pace of others, no matter what the cost to ourselves and to those around us. When that happens, we have lost our spiritual path. Our souls long to do something right but, day in and day out, we are so caught up in the same routine, that we don't know where to start. Each step seems to take us further in the wrong direction. When we reach this point, it is time to pause and try to grasp how—and, more importantly, why—we interact with other human beings.

Learning Our Spiritual Lessons
The reason that we come into contact with specific people—friends, co-workers, and bosses—is to learn a spiritual lesson from our interactions with them. Such interactions are not only learning experiences for us but also opportunities to show the spiritual path to others and to contribute our skills and talents to the universe. Similarly, when we are born into a family, each of us as a soul has chosen to be born into that particular family in order to grow spiritually. Each child brings with him or her a spiritual lesson to teach the parent and vice versa. The teaching usually has the purpose of transforming our weaker spiritual qualities—such as anger, hatred, vengefulness, and envy—into patience, humility, forgivingness and other virtues that contribute to the evolution of our souls. Our earthly journeys are thus intertwined with the spiritual journeys of others and ourselves. This is so that we can all move forward and grow spiritually.

On Earth, all children spend many hours a day at school. They educate themselves, make new friends, hold on to old friends, and sometimes stay bonded with one another throughout life. Each friend or fellow student that comes into a child's life has something to teach or to learn. This is not a coincidence but the soul's choice and part of the plan of the universe.

Similarly, when we are teenagers and adults we spend many hours in schools, universities, and other learning institutions, as well as at work. The students, teachers, and professors with whom we interact, the workplace, and the organizations for whom we work become our training ground on Earth to cultivate and sharpen our spiritual knowledge and experience. If we are arrogant, we will be placed in a situation to learn humility. If we are angry all the time, we will be placed in a situation to learn to be calm and to control our temper. If we are impatient, our situations will teach us to have faith and patience in life. If we are disrespectful, we will learn the art of respect. If we are smart, we will figure out the value of being humble in life. If we are callous and cruel, we will find ourselves in circumstances designed to show us how to be kind and compassionate in life. Whatever we have chosen to learn in this earthly life, we will face the situations necessary for our development.

From the most everyday situations we can learn the greatest lessons. Take, for instance, the experience of Tina, an administrative clerk and long-time employee in a reputable company. Tina had seen many supervisors come and go, and felt that her knowledge and experience was superior to theirs. She would resist change and did not like any of her supervisors telling her what to do. As a result, she rarely got along well with her supervisors and managers; and she was always complaining and dissatisfied. Finally, Tina turned to her mother to discuss the challenges she was facing at work. Her mother recognized Tina's pattern and advised her to adjust her behaviour—to be open to change and to listen to her supervisors. Her mother suggested that she give this a try for one month. Tina took her mother's advice and became more willing to listen and to act on suggestions from her supervisors.

She noticed that things changed quickly and that it was she who had needed to change her behavior. As a result, things went smoothly for her at work. Having learned to listen, Tina became more content, and her new attitude created a more peaceful environment.

As Tina's story suggests, each of us on a daily basis should try to contribute cooperation and peace to our particular environment, whether it is in our personal life or at work. In Tina's case, this was a fairly simple matter of a deliberate change in attitude. In other cases, the problems and possible choices may be more complex .This brings to mind the dilemma of Crystal, a clerk working in a unionized environment. She had two small kids and was the only earning member in the family, as her husband had recently lost his job.

One day at work, Crystal received a call from the Human Resources department. Another union person in a different department had lost his job due to restructuring and, because of greater seniority, was bumping Crystal from the clerk's position. Crystal had thirty days to find another job within the organization or bump another employee with less seniority than hers. Crystal was on the right spiritual path and her consciousness told her not to bump another person; meanwhile she was under constant pressure from the Human Resources representative to follow the union protocol.

Crystal did not know where to turn until she met Nick, a manager working in the same office but handling a different portfolio and managing a different team. She asked Nick to consider her for a temp or a casual job until she found something permanent. Nick was a good listener and Crystal mentioned that she was being pressured to bump someone. She also expressed her dismay that the system allowed someone to pick her name from a list and take her job, while no one apparently cared that hers was the only income supporting her whole family for the foreseeable future. She wanted the chain of injustice to stop; her higher self was against taking away someone's job and she didn't mind if she was unemployed for a short period of time.

She asked Nick how she should handle the situation. Nick advised that at times the earthly laws and spiritual laws are not in harmony and that she should follow the advice of her higher mind. Nick's affirmation of her own belief brought a sense of relief to Crystal and she left his office in a happier state of mind. At home, she told her husband that she was not bumping anyone, and her husband supported her decision. They knew times were going to be tough but they had faith in God and faith that if they were on the right spiritual path, all would be well.

A few days later, Crystal walked into Nick's office and relayed the good news that there were earthly and spiritual powers at play in her life. She was able to get a management position in the same company but in a different location. Sometimes all we need is validation from another person for taking the right spiritual action. We should therefore never not hesitate to provide that advice to help someone else go forward in their journey on Earth. Crystal's correct action helped her to find a management position and she does not even have to worry about another bumping scenario in the new job. Crystal repaid her karma with her correct action of not taking away the job of another person, even though she had lost her own job.

Crystal's experience illustrates that our proper role is to help others, even when we are caught in a system that encourages self-serving actions. Crystal rightly realized the wisdom of understanding the perspectives of others—whether they are an employee, co-worker, child, friend, parent or spouse. When we connect with people on a soul level, we grow spiritually, evolve as souls, and end bad karma.

Nick's support of Crystal, demonstrates the value of bringing out the best in other people by helping them make their journeys on Earth, and within organizations, in peace. As Nick did with Crystal, show others your true spirit, compassion, love, and kindness. Show them that you are a soul first and foremost, and thus an understanding parent, teacher, advisor, friend, spouse, and colleague. We should never be afraid to share our real life experiences with others. If we see a friend who is always angry at his own self and the universe, we should reveal our own struggles with anger and how we achieved self-control. If someone has a problem with forgiving another person, we can help by recalling our own path to forgivingness. When we share our experiences we also share our pain and lighten our burden of pain, while at the same time enlightening another soul and inspiring him or her to follow the right path on Earth.

We all should have one goal and desire in life: to bring out the best in other people. How can we serve others to help make their earthly journeys richer, more meaningful, and more inspiring? How can we bring out the best in others and put a smile on someone's face without compromising our own values and integrity, or the organizational values and integrity of where we work? How can we be committed to serve so that our soul can find peace on Earth? Every opportunity we get, we need to use it for the betterment of other human beings. Every opportunity that we get to serve others, in personal or work environments, brings us closer to another soul on Earth. Every opportunity is a step forward to advance our soul spiritually. Every opportunity brings us closer to God and keeps us connected to our higher selves.

There will be times when we are taking the right steps in our lives and acting with high consciousness but are not receiving reciprocal treatment from others. Rather than becoming dejected, we need to recall that such a situation is a spiritual test—from which we can learn and grow spiritually. If we analyze ourselves, we will typically find that we need to strengthen one of our own spiritual soul characteristics. Do not lose faith. It happens to all of us. The more we are on the spiritual path, the more spiritual tests will come our way to test our faith. This helps each of us strengthen our individual spirit. Spiritual tests are challenges that our souls need to overcome, and when we rise to the challenge with consciousness, we move one step further along the path to God's light and divine energy.

We must avoid acting unconsciously as a way of getting better treatment from others. On the contrary, in any situation in life, we need to recall our own learning experience, sit in peace and silence, and observe how someone's act has impacted us; then we take one step further and visualize the impact if we were to perform the same act on others. If our soul is spiritually developed, we will never emulate others' unconscious choices, because we have learnt the lesson, and our soul knows the difference between right and wrong. In my early years, life taught me lessons of betrayal and how betrayal can damage any relationship. When I was faced with that life-challenging situation, it brought a total awakening in my spirit and made me realize that because someone else's betrayal caused so much grief in my life, I would never deliberately take part individually or collectively in any action to betray another and cause pain and misery. I thank God for bringing that incident of betrayal into my own life. It has made me better in my spirit and more consciously driven to do the right thing.

Listening to Our Higher Minds

We all try to make conscious choices most of the time, but when we are in high pressure situations, we tend to start thinking from our physical minds. This is most likely to happen when we are irritated, upset, and low in spirit. Once we let the physical mind take precedence over the higher mind, we are at risk of doing the stupidest things, like speaking irrationally, picking fights, showing off, and exerting our power over the weak and submissive. Whenever I have listened to my physical mind and ignored my higher mind, thus making unconscious choices, trouble has always soon been waiting on my doorstep.

So, how do we start listening to our higher minds?

Staying as calm as possible in all situations is conducive to listening to our higher minds. One lesson that I have learnt in life is not to take any action when I have a conflict between my physical mind and my higher mind. If the conflict is strong and the urge to make choices with my physical mind is predominant, I focus my attention on some unrelated task. This allows time for my physical mind to cool down. I might take a walk outdoors, go to the gym, or read a book to uplift my spirit. Most of the time the answer for which I am looking is delivered in one of the chapters of the book I am reading. Meditating also helps us awaken and uplift our higher minds, so that the choices we make are conscious, fulfilling to the spirit, and good for others and the universe.

Learning to adjust to the expectations of others is another useful strategy. We can weigh what others do and say, while at the same time staying alert to the wisdom of our higher minds. In addition, we need to be patient with ourselves. Awareness more often comes in small insights rather than grand epiphanies. So we should feel comfortable with growing gradually accustomed to the voice of the higher mind, one scenario at a time. As we start listening to every nuance and whisper from our higher minds, and acting accordingly, our lives become easier.

Our own higher mind guides each of us in every phase of our lives, and the more we listen, the stronger it grows. The more we implement its advice, the better we get at listening and making conscious choices in life, for it is the higher mind, not the physical mind that governs the development of each soul. When we listen to the higher mind, we are hearing God's perspective, which is full of truth, kindness, and compassion. When we listen too much to our physical minds, we will be drawn toward selfishness, revenge, hatred, controlling behaviours, hurtfulness, and egocentricity. Remember, everything in life comes down to choice. What choices are we making in leading our lives on Earth? Are we making the right choices? Is each of our spirits filled with truth, kindness, compassion, and forgivingness? Or do we give free reign to selfishness and other destructive impulses? If we analyze our true selves, we will know the answers to these questions.

Is it too late to change in life? No. Our journeys on Earth are for leading lives of true spirituality through service to others, regardless of our circumstances and status. Now is

the time to change spiritually and to focus on the inward, on our core beliefs in life. Start the process in small steps and see the meaningful difference it will create in our bodies, minds, and spirits. Most of all, we will notice the change in how others behave toward us. We will find life meaningful, purpose driven, and full of inspiration. It will take us to the next level of happiness, which we have not previously attained in our lives.

Learning through Interactions with Other Souls on Earth

We are all connected to God and when we understand this, we love our lives. We strengthen our connection to God through spiritual growth, which we achieve through interactions with other souls. Some interactions will be pleasant, beautiful, and peaceful; some will leave dark scars in our lives. The people who scar our lives, who shake us up emotionally, and who create turmoil in our lives are often the ones who teach us important spiritual lessons. For each of us, the test is in how we react to that person and situation. How calmly do we take things in our stride and move forward? Eventually, when we have learnt the lesson and our souls have gained the wisdom, that person will either become distant from us or we will move into a better environment, a place of peace and love.

Take, for example, what happened to Jason, who was working in an office as a sales representative. The environment was pleasant, he got along well with his manager, and he loved going to work each day. His performance was excellent and his sales were outstanding in his territory. He was nominated for best salesman of the year.

When Jason's manager decided to move to another company, this left the Sales Manager position vacant, and Jason applied to fill it. The only other applicant was Chase, a cousin of the VP of Sales and Marketing. Chase was selected for the position even though he had very little sales experience and fewer qualifications than Jason. Chase was aware that Jason had applied for the same position, and after taking over as manager, he started to make life difficult for Jason. He would not give pricing exceptions for high-volume sales orders; he challenged each and every one of Jason's decisions and would not allow him to take personal time off for emergencies.

Jason was patient, and he also knew that he could not complain to management or Human Resources because it would look as though he was acting out of resentment because he did not get the Sales Manager position. As time went by, Jason continued to perform well, even though he faced hardships with Chase; the rest of the sales team, however, were dejected and demotivated by Chase's managerial style. The company's sales for the quarter took a drastic hit of 30 per cent. The board was not happy and gave Chase one more quarter to perform well and to make up for the lost sales of the preceding quarter. Chase could not bear the pressure and he left the organization. In this example, Jason had no grudge against Chase. He took his test calmly, patiently, and smilingly; and because he passed it with uncomplaining grace, he outlasted Chase in the organization.

Everything has a reason, a higher purpose. We have each chosen the journey and the pathway to spiritual development. We cannot complain. We need to have the wisdom to let anything and everything come our way that will benefit our souls. The soul never dies, and its purpose on Earth when it takes a birth or rebirth is to evolve, to improve, and most of all, to advance spiritually so that it can achieve a higher state of consciousness.

We were each created for a purpose and all our tests, training, and hardships will lead us to this mission on Earth. That is the main reason why we are born on Earth. As individuals, each of our spiritual purposes could be entirely different from those of our parents, siblings, and the rest of whole world. But each individual's purpose has a specific meaning to his or her soul. What matters the most to one person could be totally unimportant to someone else. Each soul is unique, as is its training and development. Sometimes we are placed in similar situations or groups because that is part of our soul development in our current earthly lives. Each experience will shake us but eventually shape us into better human beings and better souls. Experiences show us the path, provide wisdom, and allow us to appreciate the universe and the grace of God.

Experiences gain momentum when they are shared with others. When we share our experiences, we give the others a gift of faith and a sense of purpose in life. We convey hope and correct understanding to enable others to endure their pain and suffering on Earth. In this way, they can continue their journeys with peace and positivity. This is the case with two friends, Jenny and Veronica.

Jenny was going through a messy divorce. She was disturbed, angry, irritable, and full of hate. Veronica shared her similar divorce experience, which she had gone through ten years earlier. Now she is well settled, with a career, a loving husband, two kids, and a warm, supportive family environment. By sharing her past painful experiences, Veronica has helped Jenny understand about hate and forgiveness, and convinced her that she will receive the best in life if she is willing to let go of the pain and to forgive herself and others who have hurt her. When Veronica shared her story, it brought a ray of hope to Jenny and gave her the courage to cope with her life. The more we share our experiences to create an impact and to change another person's life for the better, the more we will progress spiritually. Sharing reflects caring. Sharing promotes bonding and the building of relationships at a soul level. Sharing helps each of us connect with our own true purpose in life.

Life is a journey filled with struggle, hope, peace, sincerity, truth, and trust. Life builds relationships and connections at soul level. Life is an adventure to be experienced to its fullest for the betterment of us all.

• • •

Inspirational Connections

- Spiritual learning is ongoing, and necessary for your soul's development.
- Your soul evolves to a higher level when you reduce your negative traits and retain or enhance your positive traits.
- Earthly and spiritual forms of learning are related but different: earthly learning involves the acquisition of formal skills; spiritual learning depends upon your interactions with other people.
- Everyday situations at home, school, and work teach the spiritual lessons that your soul needs to learn in order to evolve.
- Take every opportunity to show others the right path and to validate choices made with their higher minds.
- Listen calmly and patiently to your own higher mind.
- You are connected to God, as is every other human being; interacting with others is the way to spiritual growth.

6
Our Relationships, Our Selves

*Humankind is a knot into which
relationships are tied.*

—Antoine de Saint-Exupéry

*Love, compassion, and forgiveness
are the important things that
should be part of our daily lives.*

—Tenzin Gyatso, Dalai Lama

IN EACH OF OUR LIVES, we interact with others in different kinds of relationships—with parents, siblings, spouse, children, extended family, friends, co-workers, those we lead, and those who lead us. Our relationships bond us to one another, inspire and support us, and provide opportunities for sharing happiness, joy, grief, and sorrow. It would be absolutely impossible for us not to have any relationship with others on Earth because, as humans, need to coexist, learn, grow, and evolve as spiritual souls. Through our relationships, we learn our spiritual lessons, refine our souls, and become our true selves.

We build relationships from the time we are born. In infancy and early childhood, the individual is predominantly attached to his or her mother, father, siblings, and grandparents. As we continue to grow in age, we start building additional relationships and soul connections with our friends, extended family, and schoolmates. Relationships are fluid. We may lose some relationships or friendships, add relationships, and sometimes sacrifice one for another. In everyday life, relationships fluctuate or dissolve for various reasons: for example, relocating to a new neighborhood or moving away to pursue educational or job opportunities. In the bigger picture, our relationships shift when we have learned the lesson we need in order to evolve and repay karma. Though we may not be able to grasp what lies beyond the dynamics of routine existence, our relationships are nonetheless part of a grand plan that may extend across many lifetimes.

Current Relationships and Former Lives

In some cases, a relationship with a friend is stronger than bonds to our siblings. This could be because your friend and you were connected in previous lives and have pleasant soul memories. In other cases, a person might be closer to a grandfather than to the father, because the grandfather might be a twin soul. In a different kind of situation an employee might be drawn to a particular manager because of mutually supportive interactions in their previous lives. Each relationship has one thing in common. When the persons involved are harmoniously connected on a soul level, the relationship will flourish, and when they are at odds at soul level, the relationship will erode. Most of the time, a connection we feel to another individual is a continuation of our past life experience. If we were friendly toward another soul in a past life, we will be drawn toward that soul in the current life. If, however, the past-life relationship was full of animosity and hurtfulness, the feelings carry forward into current life and are experienced as a sense of unease with the soul that previously caused pain.

In one of his past-life readings, the psychic Edgar Cayce (1877–1945) uncovered a complex tangle of past relationships that were adversely affecting the feelings and family life of a woman named Linda. In an article entitled "Past Lives and Present Relationships" (http://www.edgarcayce.org/ps2/soul_life_past_lives.html), John Van Auken recounts the story: Linda fell in love with a man to whom she was strongly attracted; they married and had two daughters. On the surface they looked like a regular, happy family. But there was tension between husband and wife, and Linda often felt resentment toward her spouse; in addition, Linda had not bonded with her younger daughter, who was clearly attached mainly to the father. Linda's sole comfort was her older daughter, with whom she shared a close, loving relationship.

Cayce's reading attributed the tense situation to the fact that Linda's husband had been her father in their most recent previous life together, thus explaining his tendency to be controlling and her resentment. To make matters worse, the couple's younger daughter had been the father's lover in many past lives. Meanwhile the older girl had been the mother's loyal friend through many lifetimes and was continuing in her protective, supportive role. All of the residual feelings, according to Cayce, percolated at a subconscious level and caused problems in their present-day interactions. He counselled them to think of their souls and to cultivate love and positivity in order to counteract the negative baggage that had travelled with them from their past lives.

Improving Soul Connection

We do not have to resort past-life readings to sort out the tensions in our current relationships. It is enough to know that dealing with our relationship issues is crucial for the evolution of our souls. When we feel dislike for another soul in our current lives, this does not mean that we always have to feel this way. Particular souls come into our lives for a reason—to bridge the gap of love, trust, and forgiveness, and to build better relationships in our current lives. When we each succeed at establishing, or re-establishing, connection, we pay off our karma with the other soul and both can then experience the same flow of energy. The karmic connection thus evolves and blossoms into something beautiful and friendly at a soul level.

There are many situations in which current relationship tensions can be eased for the benefit of each soul involved. For example, you might find that while you love your child, the child does not seem to love you anymore. You cannot force someone to love you, but what you can do is to continue pouring out your unconditional love for your child, without clinging to any expectations that the love will be returned. A day will come when you see a change in the child's behaviour as he or she recognizes your love and responds favourably. Patience is required and you need to stay strong and positive. Conversely, some children might feel that their parents do not love them enough and that they favour other siblings. The remedy is the same as before: continue to love your parents with no expectations, and eventually the bond between you will strengthen and bloom into reciprocated love.

Some relationships might start off well but deteriorate over time. You feel as though there is no soul connection. This is because the spiritual consciousness of one soul has progressed spiritually, while the other has regressed, and the energy patterns of both souls cannot coexist in the same environment. When, for instance, two young people fall in love, they are passionate about their life together, as well as their shared work ethics, spirituality, and love. But during the course of their relationship, they begin to withdraw from one another. Possible reasons are that they are on different consciousness levels, or one might be blocking the spiritual path of the other and not allowing him or her to perform his mission on Earth.

A similar scenario can involve siblings. Despite their blood ties, siblings are born with different levels of consciousness, and you might not get along with your brother or sister. This is to the benefit of your souls, as you are all born into the family to learn from one another and to grow spiritually. Adjust your expectations of your siblings—accept that you will have both similarities and differences.

Learn to treat all your brothers and sisters with love and kindness, and I guarantee that the environment will change for you, your siblings, and the whole family. You will love to be in their company and they will love to be with you. This is the way to bond and build relationships at a soul level, resolve differences, and repay past karma.

At this point, some people might ask, "Why do I have to be kind to others when they are unkind to me?" I would answer that you know what unkindness feels like, so why would you want to inflict it on others? The wisdom that I receive from my higher mind is that we cannot control what others do, but we can control our own selves, actions, and inner negative qualities. We do not need to worry about how others act toward us, for that is not material in life—rather, we need to focus on continuing to love them despite their hurtful behaviour. If someone is unkind, you can still behave decently and eventually that person will change his attitude toward you. Remember that every unkind thought, word, or action has a karmic reaction. Do you want to acquire more karmic debt?

Souls by nature want to build loving relationships with one another, but our free will dominates our earthly choices and sometimes works against us. Some of our choices will bond relationships and some will weaken them by creating fear, anxiety, other negative feelings, and even health problems. Jeff, for example, was married and had one son, Sam. During his teen years, Sam was often difficult—rebellious, disrespectful, and dismissive of his father. Meanwhile, Jeff's health was deteriorating and the doctors discovered problems with his kidneys. They removed one of them, and for a time, Jeff managed with the remaining kidney. After a few years, it, too, failed. He waited for a transplant but was unsuccessful in finding a donor. Sam, who was by now in his late twenties, volunteered to donate a kidney to his father, as he was a perfect match for the transplant. Sam's selfless act bridged the earlier disconnection between father and son; it allowed Jeff to live for a few more years and the two were able to spend quality time together.

The Importance of Soul Connection
In order for a relationship to be meaningful and able to promote spiritual growth, those involved must be connected at a soul level. In some relationships—be they personal or professional—common interests and good communication can draw people to one another at the earthly level. But if there is no soul connection, the relationship soon loses its lustre. In some cases, if we are not vigilant, such "soulless" relationships can lead us down the wrong spiritual path, even driving us to cheat and deceive ourselves and others. Worst of all, it is not uncommon to cling to such relationships because we have no regard for our true selves. Clearly, this is not a desirable kind of relationship. When you are trying to decide if a particular relationship is healthy, do not seek the answer from the physical mind. Instead, sit in silence and let insight flow to you from your higher mind. Relationships that help us change negative characteristics are relationships worth building and maintaining for life, because the other person is looking out for our best interests and wants us to progress spiritually.

At times, our own souls will sabotage relationships that are drawing us down in spirit and preventing us from following the right spiritual path. Our souls find ways of showing us the true colours of the other person, so that we start wondering whether we want even to start, let alone to maintain, this particular relationship. For example, suppose you get the opportunity to be interviewed for your dream job, a position that would give you absolute power to manage your department. You know you are qualified, with the necessary skill set and experience, but during the interview, as though you cannot help it, you find yourself saying things that you know will put the interviewer off and guarantee that you will not be hired. What happened in there? You might ask yourself later. The answer is that your soul sabotaged the interview process because, had you gotten the job, you would have been forced to misuse your power and you would have fallen spiritually. The soul knows what is good for your spirit, whether it is a job or a personal relationship.

Love—the Essence of Relationships and Life
Love and its companions—trust, faith, patience, and commitment—build relationships. The same truth applies in both personal life and the work environment. Relationships are not mere accidents—we as souls have chosen, and volunteered to build, these relationships prior to being born on Earth. Spiritual growth is dependent on our relationships and how we serve, interact, and coexist within them. For a relationship to flourish, we need to provide total and unconditional commitment toward interacting effectively with the other person. We need to take responsibility for our own role in the relationship and create a bond of trust and loyalty. Above all, we need to understand that our true purpose is to offer genuine love and affection to the other person.

Megan and Tony are exemplars of the ideal approach to relationships. They are happily married, love each other, and always strive to do the right thing in life. They have unconditional faith in God and believe that they will always be looked after as long as they are on the spiritual path. They are content that they have a comfortable and happy life, even though they don't have great material wealth. Like everyone else, they face life challenges but always look to divine help and guidance for the strength to deal with their problems. They understand that true love means confronting difficulties together while helping each other grow spiritually and realize their purpose in life—this is true spiritual connection. Megan and Tony's experience shows that it is easier to build a healthy relationship when both partners are following the spiritual path and making conscious choices in life.

Megan and Tony are friendly with Terri and Lloyd who are their next door neighbours. Lloyd is always thinking of making more money and achieving materialistic wealth. Terri, his wife, on the other hand, is already content with what they have and is always looking for avenues by which to follow the spiritual path. Lloyd's behaviour is not helping her grow spiritually and they have frequent differences. All of this creates a rift in their relationship. Terri wants to change her consciousness, whereas Lloyd wants to elevate his status in society. When two partners have such different levels of consciousness, their energy levels are going to clash, making it difficult to build and maintain a healthy relationship; they will tend to drift away from each other at a soul level. The spiritual choices that you make jointly to build your relationship are the choices that help you connect, and stay connected, at a soul level. These choices also help you to be more understanding, calm, and patient in dealing with life challenges on Earth.

If we endeavour to be giving, compassionate, kind, and selfless, we will be better able to understand the pain and suffering of others. And if we are open to listening to the problems faced by other people, then we are equipping ourselves to build a peaceful and harmonious relationship with any other human being on Earth. When a young woman, Sophia, was pregnant with her second child, her aunt provided just such a role model.

Things were tough in Sophia's life. She and her husband could manage when they had one child, but the family income was not enough to support a second one. They did not even know how they would be able to pay the doctors' fees. Sophia had an aunt who was close to her and her family. The aunt was known for her empathy and wise guidance when it came to handling life challenges. She advised Sophia to be calm and patient. There was no need for fear—for, as long as she was on the spiritual path, God and the universe would provide. Sophia listened to her aunt's advice and put her complete faith in God. Her aunt helped them pay for medical expenses, and three days before the child was born, her husband delivered the good news that he had been promoted. Sophia and her husband were pleased with what God had provided them in life and grateful for an aunt who restored their faith and trust in God.

If, however, we are indifferent to the needs of other human beings, any relationships we take part in are at risk of eroding and eventually ceasing to exist. If we put ourselves first, then we are apt to feel that we can only commit to a relationship if the other person defers to us or becomes the one to change. This makes for an unequal relationship that will eventually falter. To ensure the equilibrium of any relationship, each of us has to be giving and willing to let go of our own happiness or needs. This generally holds true but is particularly crucial in times of crisis. Some people, unfortunately, only learn this after it is too late.

Two sisters, Polly and Angela, were both career oriented and ambitious. They both had good jobs and prosperous lifestyles. Polly was content with her life and always made time for her family. Angela, on the other hand, was overly ambitious and perpetually discontented. She put in increasingly longer hours to achieve career goals and to make more money. She had little time for anything but work. One day she received the sad news that her mother was very ill and had only a few months to live. Angela didn't take the situation seriously and continued her heavy work schedule. After a few weeks, the mother's condition worsened, and Polly phoned to urge Angela to come to the hospital. But Angela was too involved at work and promised to come as soon as she had completed her project. It was not to be: Angela soon received another phone call from her sister, informing her that their mother had passed away.

Angela was shocked and upset that she had been so involved with work that she couldn't make time for her mom and had lost precious moments that could never be brought back. Her discontent and obsessive need for career success had cost her dearly—distancing her from family, from love, and from most other spiritual aspects of life.

The principles that make for successful family relationships also apply in the workplace. In order to build a foundation for better, more unified working relationships, all of us need to understand that each and every employee in the organization is equal. No one is superior or inferior. We are born from the same source and Creator. We work for the same organization and the only difference that sets us apart from one another is that we are at different levels in the organization because of our skill sets and work experience. A higher title does not signify that we are spiritually superior or more evolved. A higher title does not give us the right to be rude, arrogant, and unkind. A higher title does not give us the right to exert undue and unjust authority to make the other person bend to our whims and fancies. A higher title is meaningless if it does not symbolize our commitment to God and his purpose for our lives, and the only way we can fulfill this purpose is to be kind, compassionate, loving, just, and fair in all respects.

At times we become disengaged from building and maintaining productive working relationships, because we have our own corporate goals and objectives. We can become too engrossed in achieving the bottom line, maximizing profits, creating a return on investment, and promoting efficiency within the organization. As a result, we neglect to nurture our relationships with co-workers. We lose our spiritual balance, and this carries over into our private lives. We fail to engage with friends and family and with what brings us inner joy and happiness in our lives. We forget the basic principle that only when we connect can we build understanding and caring relationships, in which each person serves the other person's best interest and successful journey on Earth.

The basic foundation for building better relationships is to admire the positive qualities of each and every person. This is not difficult when we are in a healthy and loving relationship with a spouse or partner. It comes naturally to accept each other's faults and to focus on the positive qualities that each individual brings to the relationship. Similarly, when we overlook the minor weaknesses in our children, friends, parents, family members, employees, or colleagues, we are contributing to the health of the relationships, because we are appreciating the importance of the hard work, commitment, help, unconditional support, and assistance that others bring into our lives. The earlier that we realize in our earthly journey that those with whom we interact are the source of our own success, the more meaningful will be all our relationships and the greater the benefits we will reap for ourselves.

There will be times, however, when we could compromise our own integrity by ignoring the faults of others. We might have a sibling or a child who is on the wrong path. For example, he is having problems with the law and could be a bad influence on siblings or other children. What is our role when we are faced with such a situation in life? Difficult though it might be, we must strive to remain steadfast in our love for the wrongdoer while, at the same time, firmly leading him back onto the right path. For, objectionable though his attitude and behaviour might be, he is vulnerable and needs us. If we abandon him, the situation could worsen as others could take undue advantage of his weakness and your lack of love toward him. This could drive him further down the wrong path until it is too late to save his soul. Persist in your support, no matter what resistance he gives you or taunts he hurls. It is your duty to do your utmost to help him, love him, and set him back on track.

Relationships are often served better when we listen more and talk less. Listening allows others to express their emotions. It enables us to understand the depth of the problem from our higher minds and to make purely selfless decisions in the best interest of other people and the universe. On the other hand, when we do speak, we need to be clear and precise in our communication. Together, clarity of communication and empathic listening are manifestations of love. They open the doors of consciousness, enabling us to see the meaning and beauty that surround us in the universe.

Extending Love in the Family and at Work
Because we are all individuals with differing talents and personalities, it takes love to create a bond among us. Most importantly, we need to love each and every member of our families. When we make each and every member feel loved, valued, and appreciated, and when we go out of our way to help and serve them, we please our own souls. We might face hurt, hardships, and rejections from people we love, but that is all a part of being born on Earth, accepting what comes our way, and leading peaceful lives. And the benefits not only accrue to others but also to ourselves. As the Chinese philosopher Lao Tzu said, "Being deeply loved by someone gives you strength, while loving someone deeply gives you courage."

What applies in family relationships is also transferrable to our working lives. Pleasant and productive working relationships cannot be built on fear, abuse of power, manipulation, and deceit. They also cannot be created overnight by attending a workshop. We can best strengthen our workplace interactions by committing ourselves to extending and promoting such loving qualities as trust, loyalty, integrity, and mutual respect. These will achieve much higher results than intimidation and domination.

We can begin by asking ourselves what we as human beings, employees, and leaders bring to our working environments. Are people happy to be around us and to interact with us? Are they willing to drop what they are doing to spend time with us? Or do they prefer to act busy and convey the unspoken message that they want to be left alone? We need to learn to take a hint and work toward making our presence worthy of acceptance. Whether we are in subordinate or managerial positions, we need to cultivate empathy for the challenges that everyone faces in the workplace. To do so is to listen to others' concerns, to act with understanding and supportiveness, and thus to create harmonious and productive environments that inspire bosses and employees alike to do their best for themselves, their coworkers, and the organization as a whole.

In all spheres of life, what we give out in love returns to us in even greater measure. As we extend our love to everyone else, we will receive more and more of the same in life. The universe will return our love, kindness, and compassion tenfold. Hate no one, for hatred eats up our souls to such an extent that the individual lives in a continuous state of misery. The more we develop and practice loving qualities, the stronger our souls become and the happier and more peaceful we are in our earthly relationships.

• • •

Inspirational Connections

- Humans need meaningful relationships on Earth in order to evolve as spiritual souls.
- Relationship tensions are part of a larger design for the betterment of your soul.
- Ease tensions and improve soul connection through love, trust, patience, kindness, and forgiveness; do not expect immediate reciprocity.
- A relationship can only teach you spiritual lessons when you have a soul connection with the other person(s) involved.
- Healthy relationships at the soul level are the foundation for earthly contentment, spiritual growth, and the evolution of the soul.
- Love strengthens soul connection and is the key to the success of all meaningful relationships.

7
Our Spiritual Trainers

*The role of the spiritual teacher is not
to impress with words, but rather to
simply remind us of who we really are.*

—Dean Jackson

OUR SPIRITUAL TRAINERS come in many forms. Typically, they are people that we interact with in our daily lives. More often than not, our best teachers are the ones that challenge us the most. While we mainly learn from those with whom we closely interact, our trainers can also be role models that we only encounter in passing or observe from a distance. Finally, in a sense, our higher minds are our ultimate spiritual trainers, because they help us process the lessons we learn from relationships and role models. Through our spiritual trainers, we learn of soul connection, tolerance, and peace—and thus we come to know our own souls.

Spiritual Trainers That Challenge Us

Why should it be that the people who irritate us the most or bring out the worst in us become our spiritual trainers in our earthly lives? The answer is that if we are only building on our positive spiritual qualities, we are not working on our negative traits. In order to help us move forward and tackle spiritual challenges on Earth, refine our souls, and correct our spiritual weaknesses, these trainers walk into our lives. If we ignore our spiritual challenges or resist a specific trainer, we will be faced with a similar challenge through a different trainer until we overcome our weaknesses, develop, and move ahead in life.

The role of a trainer is not only to teach us but to learn from us. Imagine, for example, that you have a child who is constantly irritating you in petty matters and driving you up the wall—testing your patience, anger management capacity, and mental stability. He is born to train you to overcome your own negative qualities. How well do you accept this training? Do you learn something? Do you accept the training with a smile and take it in your stride? Do you take it as a challenge to improve and grow spiritually? Are you able to keep your mind cool and temper at bay, despite all the irritation that is thrown at you? Can you control your rage and urges to lash out, fight back, and speak harshly? These are all training points to consider, and the more you can answer yes to the questions, the more you are growing spiritually.

In this kind of scenario, your spiritual trainer is also learning something from you. He or she learns that irritating others does not gain anything and a wake-up call sounds in his or her higher mind. The child begins to see that maintaining peace is a desirable way of life. He or she feels the need to change, and seeing a change in you inspires a transformation of attitude for the better as the child learns to control his or her mind. In other words, the two of you have crossed paths in your earthly journeys and have done so in peace. The way is now paved for you both to move toward common spiritual goals in life.

I remember a comparable episode from my own experience. One day I came home from work and my son (who is now grown up) returned from school at the same time. He had gone through a rough day and was not in good spirits. He needed someone to vent his frustration on. While I patiently listened to him, he uttered some harsh words, saying things that he did not really mean. Mindful of his discouraging day, I kept quiet. Within minutes he realized what he had done and came to say sorry. I accepted his apology and smiled at him.

He asked me one question: "How could you be that calm when I said all those mean things to you?"

I replied, "I learnt the art from the best teacher in this world."

He tried a few names on me and I kept shaking my head, no. He eventually coaxed me to name the teacher who had taught me to be calm and patient. I smiled and replied, "I learnt it from you. Don't you remember?"

He and I both realized that we had touched each other in a spiritual way. We smiled, hugged each other, and moved on to enjoy the rest of our evening in peace and harmony.

The children in our lives are there to teach us lessons. They know our weak points and will capitalize on them, which can be very upsetting and draining. In my situation, my child was born to teach me patience and calmness. He was also born to build a bond of love between us at a soul level. I learnt from life-challenging experiences that I cannot change his behaviour, but I can influence it by not reacting to his comments and by controlling my anger. I can send him a message of patience, and continue to love him in spite of his negative attitude, in the conviction that he will change. When we handle life experiences with grace, calmness, humility, and understanding, we become examples to other souls to do the same.

Although dealing with our children can be trying, the irritation or frustration is always mediated by love. Dealing with a difficult co-worker or boss, on the other hand, can be particularly challenging because love is not typically part of the equation of our relationship. It is therefore all too easy to feel irritable, impatient, angry or even indifferent. It helps to remember that every employee and leader has something to learn from one another in order to grow spiritually.

Sometimes, in order to deal with difficult working relationships, we may need to adjust our ego-driven earthly values and make a determined effort to draw upon our spiritual values. At other times, we may simply observe a negative quality in someone else and privately vow, "I will not fall into that trap." Appealing to the higher self is the way to avoid making a comparable turn to the negative. Instead of bemoaning the fact that we are forced to deal with negativity at work, we each need to ask our higher selves, what must I do to learn and grow spiritually in this situation? How can I help the other person learn his or her spiritual path?

This kind of situation is a spiritual test, and we pass it when we keep our tempers, maintain self-control, and react with patience. We pass when we are generous in extending our support and present ourselves as pillars of strength that others can rely on in their times of stress and distress.

Every such spiritual test that we pass evolves our souls to the next level and strengthens our soul connection to the other person involved. We are thus at peace, on a higher spiritual plane than before, and one step closer to God.

Sometimes our relationships with our spiritual trainers last only for a short period of time—just long enough to bring us hope, uplift our spirits, and get us back on the spiritual path. Other relationships might have the sole purpose of teaching one specific lesson and, once we complete the spiritual circle with another soul by learning the lesson, we might then move ahead in our earthly journeys on our own. In some cases, however, the spiritual awakening might be of such magnitude that we bond with the other soul, and stay connected with one another for life.

The Wisdom of Letting Go

Sometimes, spiritual trainers with whom we have uneasy relationships inadvertently teach us a lesson about not fighting losing battles. Perseverance is not always a virtue, while, on occasion, letting go is. There may be instances when you desperately want to maintain a relationship but the other person is doing everything in his or her power to consciously break the relationship. There could be various reasons. Perhaps the person has done something wrong to you intentionally and continues to do so each day, while you remain unaware of the situation. The other person has not the courage to openly admit the truth and simply wants to end the relationship. He or she is in a constant struggle between the physical mind and the higher mind. It is time to let go, so that you, too, can move on.

There may also be scenarios in which another person has done wrong to you but is under the assumption that you are not aware of it. But you, in fact, know the truth from other sources. You do not speak up because you are hurt, or the bond of trust has been broken, or you have been betrayed and your love replaced with that of someone else. In addition, with your silence, you may be trying to hold on to the relationship. But it may also be that, whether short-lived or of long standing, the relationship has served its purpose and helped you repay some karma. Or maybe, it was simply never meant to be. Either way, let it go. Let's not cling to relationships because, to enjoy life, we must not only be free from worldly attachment to materialistic objects but also free from attachment to people that do not reciprocate our feelings or contribute to our spiritual growth

An Exemplary Role Model

In addition to those who teach us as we interact with them, there are others whom we do not know personally, but who set an example that shines widely and touches many. A role model of both personal and organizational generosity is Ratan Tata, board chairman (1991-2012) of the Tata Group of companies group whose "flagship" is the Taj Mahal Hotel, in Colaba, Mumbai, next to the Gateway of India. When the hotel was targeted in a terrorist attack on November 26, 2008, Ratan Tata and Tata Group of companies responded decisively and generously. For all categories of employee, including even casual workers who had completed just one day of service, they provided psychological help and covered 1600 employees under the Employee Outreach program, providing food, water, sanitation, counselling, and first aid. To cut down on bureaucracy, each employee was assigned an individual mentor who acted as a representative and clearance authorizer for any assistance that the employee needed. People who were not a part of the organization but were victims of the attack—such as railway employees, police staff, and pedestrians—were provided with a subsistence allowance for six months.

Ratan Tata and Tata Group of companies also paid the medical expenses for a vendor's four-year-old daughter, who had been wounded by bullets during the attack. They further committed to providing education for life for all forty six children who were the victims of the terrorism. The dependants of every deceased employee were paid lump-sum settlements and benefits that included education for children and dependants anywhere in the world; loans were waived and counselling for life provided.

This amazing story touched my heart as I thought about the compassion generated at both an organizational and a soul level. Truly, Mr. Ratan Tata must have been guided spiritually by the forces of the universe or a higher power to bring about such a positive change in the lives of the affected employees. The selfless assistance rendered was inspiring and showed other human beings how the power we are entrusted with on Earth can be used to serve others. The soul relationship that Mr. Ratan Tata and Tata Group of companies established with so many will be long remembered, not only by the families of the victims but throughout India and abroad.

Our Higher Minds

Our higher minds are always working in conjunction with our role models and others from whom we learn spiritual lessons. In this sense, our higher minds are our single most constant teachers. We build earthly relationships by loving and caring for others; similarly, we come to know ourselves better when we love and care for our own souls. We do so by listening to our higher minds or, as some people say, the voice of conscience.

The soul grows spiritually when we follow, act on, and implement the higher voice of our conscience, which guides us in our day-to-day lives, every second and every minute. It is our constant companion throughout our lives and linked to us for eternity. Each action that we choose to implement after listening to our higher minds brings us closer to God and consciousness. The more we are attuned to listening to our higher minds, the greater is our connection to our own souls. Our souls can thus guide us to lead with integrity, abide by our values, honour our true commitments, control our negative desires and feelings, and show us the path to living with consciousness. That is our soul's commitment to each of us.

Our responsibility is to honour the guidance of the soul so that we can clearly see and follow the spiritual path, overcome all obstacles, and lead fulfilling lives that bring us peace. The strength to do all this comes to us when we start listening to our higher minds. We face all our earthly challenges with patience and positivity. Our physical minds come to understand that each event is for our own spiritual advancement, and that we are here to fulfill God's plan on Earth.

Our Spiritual Lessons

Soul connections. The story of Ratan Tata, and the generosity of Tata Group of companies in a time of trouble, illustrates the importance of selfless acts, compassion, kindness, and love as the way to expand our soul connections. Our roles on Earth may be different, but we still have the potential to be connected to one another at a soul level. To forget this potential is to forget our own spiritual values and journeys as spiritual beings in physical bodies.

Tolerance. One of the great lessons we can learn from our earthly relationships is to cultivate tolerance. Some might ask, why should I tolerate certain people if I don't feel like it? At the earthly level, tolerance is often a practical necessity. For example, parents tolerate their children's arrogant behaviour because they love their children and want to be loved in return. Friends tolerate one another because they value their friendship and are therefore willing to overlook each other's faults. And employees often tolerate their bosses simply because they need a job.

Tolerance does not signify that you are meek, cowardly, or weak. Tolerance often requires a great deal of courage, patience, and calmness. Tolerance equals lovingness in any relationship. At the spiritual level, tolerance means acceptance of any situation or person that comes our way to teach us life lessons on Earth. When we are tolerant in this way, we are flowing with the universe. We are not fighting back with our physical minds but, rather, we are in harmony with nature. The universe provides a problem so that we can learn and grow spiritually, and every problem that presents itself widens into a wonderful path, along which—if we are positive and tolerant—our souls progress. When we tolerate another human being, we take the first step toward peace. We relinquish our urge to be right in any given situation, and stop arguing and complaining. This creates peaceful and loving energy that radiates to those around us and brings tranquillity to our own spirit.

Peace. The ego feeds our needs, not our spirits. The key to generating peace is to rise above ego and strive for greater spiritual consciousness. This consciousness is pure and radiant.

When we start listening to the peaceful voice of our higher minds and ignore the egoistic voice of our physical minds, our lives tend to flourish in all directions. Peace comes to us when we least expect it. Friends provide a helping hand when we need it. Problems that have been persisting in our lives are resolved. We don't see life's pain and suffering; instead we view life as a spiritual journey, through which we grow in harmony. We generate peace, radiate it, and receive it back in return. .

Inner peace makes life more meaningful, calm, and spiritually satisfying. Each day brings more inner joy, as we purposefully serve others, share, grow, and learn from one another. We strive ever harder to inspire those with whom we live and work. We become more attuned to nature—the gentle beauty of a tree, the fragrance of the air we breathe. In such moments of appreciation, it can seem as though Earth stands still, allowing us to see the universe and feel the Higher Power within us, as peace, happiness, kindness, compassion, and humility flow into and around us from all directions.

Inner peace fosters gratitude and enhances insight. We are grateful for the life we have today and for what lies ahead tomorrow. Yesterday becomes distant. Fame, glory, and material success are no longer the goals that we want to achieve. Instead, we commit to spreading love, kindness, and supportiveness to others. We see God's hand in everything and feel the spiritual light illuminating our souls, and guiding us toward the greater cause of God Almighty.

• • •

Inspirational Connections

- Your spiritual trainers are people you interact with in your daily life, role models, and your own higher mind.
- You learn from those with whom you are in relationships and, in turn, you teach them; this is especially true in challenging relationships.
- You pass your spiritual tests at home and at work when you behave with the necessary love, patience, generosity, calmness, and self-control.
- Your relationships teach tolerance; role models demonstrate how to increase your soul connections; and your higher mind shows you the way to peace.
- With each lesson learned and test passed, you are one step closer to God.

8
Earthly Power and the Power Within

*The day the power of love overrules the
love of power, the world will know peace.*

—*Mahatma Gandhi*

POWER IS A GIFT from God, one with which we are all entrusted. Since power resides with the individual, it is the responsibility of everyone to make conscious choices that will lead to making a meaningful difference in the lives of others. Whether we are using earthly power or the inner power that connects us to our higher minds, the ideal is to exercise the free will that each of us possesses in order to generate goodness and kindness.

Earthly, or External, Power

In our earthly world, external power may be bestowed on an individual through work, government, or community organizations. Typically, the higher an individual's title and position in an organization, the greater the power he or she wields. External power is often accompanied by material benefits and an exaggerated sense of pride that "I am the boss," "I have the power," and "I can achieve the goals by any means, fair or otherwise." Since each person possesses free will, they can choose to use their external power for good and selfless ends or they can use it for ego-driven, selfish purposes. The former kind of choice is conscious and comes from the soul; the latter kind is the product of the physical mind and ego. Unconscious choices stem mainly from our own fears, insecurities, inadequacies, and lack of self-worth. Power is sublime and pure if used in the right manner, and tainted if used for selfish interests and personal gain. Using power to dominate others by instilling fear, or being controlling and manipulative, is wrong.

People who make conscious choices when using their power are aligned with their own spirits. Their spirits do not allow them to misuse power at the expense of others. These individuals have a lot of self-worth and are confident in their actions, because they spring from a soul level. People make unconscious choices because they are weak minded, feel insecure and inadequate, and have low self-worth. Controlling others gives them a false sense of security and satisfies their egos. The need to control and the need to please others are generated from our own inadequacies because our spirits are not refined or in harmony with nature.

Some people will use power wisely by making conscious choices, while others will do the opposite. An unconscious use of power is to take credit for someone else's work and inspirational ideas. For example, your colleague has proposed new procedures and technology to enhance efficiency and savings within the department, but you present the initiative to the top executives as your own and do not give credit to the employee who contributed the idea and drafted the proposal. The ego gratification for the one who misleads yields no direct benefit for the organization. Conversely, power used consciously and coupled with truthfulness can bring meaningful results that will advance the organization, employees, and teams.

Use of External Power—Shifting Your Consciousness
The use of external power in alignment with the spirit originates from a soul level. Power exercised this way—that is, consciously—arises from pure and selfless intentions. The resulting actions will inevitably produce a positive outcome. A case in point is the experience of two brothers, Ray and Alan, whose father owned two pizza franchises.

When their father died, Ray was twenty-four and Alan, only nineteen. The distribution of assets was not uniform; Ray inherited 100 per cent of one franchise and 50 per cent of the other, leaving Alan as owner of only half a franchise. Alan was upset about the uneven distribution of assets and, as a result, harboured some distrust and resentment toward his brother. Ray could not handle both the businesses alone and allowed Alan to manage the second franchise. Luck favoured Alan, and his franchise was making more money than Ray's. Although they loved each other, the brothers knew that the inheritance was not allowing their relationship to flourish.

By unfortunate circumstances, Ray fell sick and had to be hospitalized. He was advised to have complete rest for a period of nine months. Alan took control of both businesses and made sure that the accounting was up-to-date. He regularly deposited all of Ray's share faithfully into his bank account. When Ray recovered and joined the business again, he realized that his younger brother had made a lot of management changes and things were working well at both franchises. The franchise that Ray owned was performing better than it had when he was managing it.

Ray took some time to digest all the changes and go through the financial records. He now saw that his dad had done an injustice to Alan. Making a conscious decision, Ray called the family lawyer and instructed him to allocate 100 per cent of the second franchise to Alan. Ray's soul realized that in times of need, and when he was sick, the only person he could rely on was Alan. He also recognized that his wealth had no value if he did not have his brother's love. What had started as an unequal distribution of wealth, with resultant resentment, now flourished as a healthy relationship between two souls.

The Power to Make a Difference
As Ray's actions show, we all have the power to make a difference in this world. Sometimes, however, we hesitate to take appropriate action because, in our insecurity, we worry about how others will perceive us. This groundless worry is never a valid excuse for failing to do the right thing.

Making a difference starts with small steps. When a person comes to us for help, we can listen, counsel, provide direction, and confirm his or her beliefs, approach, and attitude in life. We can, in other words, be compassionate and empathetic toward another's suffering or turmoil. We each have this kind of power to put a smile on someone's face, even to change someone's life. We can use it to do something selfless, to generate love and kindness. The greatest reason to use our power to make a difference is because God has bestowed it upon us for the betterment of all human beings on Earth.

Power is infinite. If we look at it from God's point of view, everyone has power in some form or other, and how we use it is what counts. What is our intent in using our power? What purpose are we trying to serve? Is it selfless or selfish? Are we simply trying to please someone or to make a meaningful difference in the lives of others? Is the aim to generate peace, love, harmony, and friendship or is it to create distortion and discord? Do we wish to fulfill our egos and earthly goals or to serve others without expecting anything in return?

The power to contribute selflessly is greater than the power to snatch something for our selfish needs. In the end it comes down to the power to love exceeding the power to hate. Exercising the power to love leads us toward creativity, fulfillment, and peace in life, while choosing the power to hate leads us down a path of destruction. The power to understand someone has a greater meaning than the power to dismiss someone. The reason we are in a position of power is because we were born to serve. When we use our power consciously, we are being true to ourselves and to God. Leadership at this level makes a difference because we are helping others and inspiring them to follow in our footsteps.

If, however, we allow the ego to dictate our actions, we forget our true purpose in life, our connection with God, our higher minds, and the interests of our fellow human beings. If we carry on in this way, we will develop self-hatred as emptiness engulfs mind, body, and spirit. This can become a vicious circle if we continue to ignore our higher selves. The ego will grow ever stronger until it—and the accompanying emptiness—dominates every aspect of ourselves and our lives. True leadership is not mainly about ego and retaining power at the expense of others. It is a gift to be used consciously and wisely, with humility, sincerity, truthfulness, and respect.

There have been times when I wondered why I was working with a specific organization. Each time I posed that question to my higher self, I received the same answer. I have something to learn here that will enable me to evolve and to grow spiritually. Each organization brings us leaders and employees who will teach us life lessons for our journeys on Earth. Some will teach us how to embrace the unknown. Others will teach us how to control our anger, irritation, and impatience. Some will teach us humility, while others will help us expand our skills and creativity. Elsewhere we might learn the art of silence or how to fight for a just cause. Still other situations might school us in forgiveness and bring new friends into our lives. We might find peace and happiness in some experiences, and pain and sorrow in others. At all times, we need to subordinate our egos in order to distinguish ourselves, not merely as leaders or employees of organizations but as spirit beings, self-empowered to make a positive difference in the world.

The Power to Share and Serve

When selflessly shared, power multiplies; it returns back to us in abundance. No one knew this better than Jean, a branch manager in one of the top five banks in Canada. A woman with a high spiritual consciousness, she believed that she had the power to make a difference in the lives of her team and other colleagues. Jean would always encourage people to work to the best of their abilities and to move ahead.

Adriana joined Jean's branch as a Customer Service Representative. She was a hard worker; she learned all the processes and was promoted to Financial Service Representative. As she did for everyone changing positions, Jean made sure that Adriana's predecessor trained her perfectly and that Adriana was fully supported in her new role. Jean considered her managerial power to be a God-given gift and also never forgot that others had helped her when she was struggling in her career. Her generous attitude inspired others to continue the chain of kindness, to help others in life, and to show by example how to use power wisely.

Rita is another manager working for the same banking institution as Jean. But her philosophy is different. She will only promote someone if there is a political benefit and if she can use her connections for her own career advancement. Rita and Jean exemplify opposing soul characteristics; self-interest versus the gift of looking after the interests of others.

Sharing flows from our inner hearts. It is spontaneous. It is a trait of givers, not receivers. It has only one need: to help others grow and lead fulfilling lives. Sharing acknowledges the fact that we are all connected at a soul level and that someone, somewhere, once helped us, in this or a previous life. The connection becomes all the stronger when we share our joys and sorrows. Each shared story has a meaning not only for our lives but also carries transformative potential for listeners who are going through painful moments in their own lives. Sharing reflects wisdom, peace, and compassion for humanity in general.

When we share with a pure motive, we will be rewarded not with wealth but with grace from God, and that grace will flow through our lives, enriching them with meaning and fulfillment. Our acts of sharing will not likely make us rich and famous but we will certainly grow in spiritual wealth and wisdom—which is the very reason we are all born on Earth.

Avoiding Abuse of Power

When we are in positions of earthly power and operating from the physical mind, it can be tempting to let the ego take over and to give our negative qualities free reign. The impulse to hurt someone mentally, or to put someone down, comes to the forefront and, left uncontrolled, harms not only others but ourselves. When we are in a position of power, we may feel that we are always right and be unwilling to listen to anyone else's suggestions or advice, even though doing so would be in the in the best interest of other people and the organization.

We need to be alert at all times to the temptations that spring from the physical mind and ego, and advise us to do wrong just because we can. We need to choose our actions wisely, because if we fail to do so, we can create grief, anxiety, depression, and physical illness for ourselves and for those who are at the receiving end of our negative actions. The best tactic when we are faced with an urge to make unconscious use of our power is to slow down. We need to take a moment to reflect on what we are planning to do and to anticipate the repercussions, not only for ourselves but for others. It is helpful in such a situation to ask ourselves the following questions:

> Am I considering this action to defend my ego, position, power, and authority?
> Is this action justified and required?
> Is there a peaceful way of resolving this issue?

We must never neglect to explore options that originate from our higher, not our physical, minds. Decisions made in the heat of the moment are rarely effective and typically regretted at a later stage. The action to take is the one that will generate peace and harmony for us, our teams, and the organizations we lead. What is the sense of retaining a job, authority, and power when we are not happy in body, mind, and spirit?

When we find ourselves in dilemmas and unable to shake off the ego, it helps to meditate—to sit in silence and to listen attentively to our higher selves. I guarantee that if you take just a few minutes to meditate, you will always avoid taking unconscious advantage of your power.

As leaders with power, we each have a responsibility to our employees, teams, and organization to endeavour to tap into our higher mind. We need to remember that we are also spirit beings with a responsibility toward other human beings. Let us not make our decisions or our life journeys filled with ego, self-centredness, and cynicism. For the good of our co-workers, our organizations, and our own souls, we must simply cultivate the habit of listening to the quiet counsel of our higher selves. This, and a willingness to change, will always take us down the right and conscious path.

Real power lies in being kind, compassionate, and loving to all human beings on Earth. The shift in consciousness is evolving. People who are acting consciously are in positions of power all over the world to help spread positivity and peace. But elevating consciousness is not just the responsibility of a select group of developed souls. We all have the power to follow the guidance of our higher minds and to become part of a larger movement for change. Through our individual actions we can together shift the collective consciousness and foster peace, dignity, equality, and love all over the world. In this way, we not only serve others but also the universe. We all have the choice to contribute by using our own power wisely. I am confident that you will join the collective force in the universe by conscious creating your own dignified, loving, and respectful environment.

Inner Power—the Connection to Our Higher Minds
Inner power is our link to our higher minds and enables us to make the right choices in life. When we use our inner power we grow in contentment, gratitude, and happiness because these qualities spring from the higher mind as a result of our making conscious choices. In other words, we always have the power to choose to be content, grateful, and happy.

Inner power is divine—in contemporary parlance, it is the real you. The problem begins when we choose to ignore our inner power and, hence, our higher minds— usually because we prefer to receive the instant gratification that our egos offer. The way to avoid this pitfall and to build inner power is a three-step process:

1. We must always strive to do what is spiritually right— even, or perhaps especially, if there is no earthly gain.

2. We must guide others to the right spiritual path.
3. We must continuously strive to be in harmony with our souls— by being selfless and compassionate.

When we strengthen our own inner power, we also strengthen our connection to the higher mind—a connection that, in turn, helps us to raise the level of our individual consciousness.

The Power of the Higher Mind
The higher mind guides us in all our actions in life. It is a mechanism that protects us from negativity and makes us aware of what helps or hinders us spiritually. Communing with our own higher mind is thus the main way that we can uplift our individual consciousness. According to what we think, speak, and do, our individual consciousness changes constantly, becoming higher or lower. The consciousness draws each of us toward the life experiences required for our own soul to improve. Our consciousness is the truth. It is the path that shows us light and uplifts the spirit.

Because of the connection between the higher mind and consciousness, it is crucial that we tap into our higher minds as we go about our daily lives. Imagine, for example, that you have constant fights with one of your loved ones. He may be the one to pick the fight for no apparent reason, but you add to the problem by responding. No lesson is learnt and you have not shifted your consciousness. If, however, you had paused to listen to your higher mind, you would not have fought back. You would have stayed calm, controlled your temper, and brought peace into the environment. You would also have raised your consciousness.

Consciousness cannot be elevated to its highest level overnight. But we progress each and every time that we stifle anger, refrain from arguing a point, and maintain calmness. Thus we improve in stages as we listen to the higher mind and let it guide each of us to right action and enhanced consciousness.

The Power of Free Will to Develop Our Souls
God has empowered each individual with free will. This means that, without any boundaries or conditions, we are at liberty to make right and conscious choices in life in order to evolve our souls. Free will guarantees that we are not limited in our thinking and ability to see all the options in our lives. Free will affords us two fundamental choices: either we can make conscious choices that draw us closer to God; or we can listen to the physical mind instead of the higher mind, make unconscious choices, and alienate our souls from God. If we make the second choice, we can end up adrift in anger, hatred, revenge, jealousy, selfishness, and other destructive powers that potentially reside within us. When we use these destructive powers, we not only harm others, but we reduce our own level of consciousness to a low point.

Of the two basic choices that we are free to make it is obvious which one is the most desirable for the betterment of our souls. But the question remains, how do we use our free will to make the right choices in life? The simple formula for productively exercising the power of free will is to consider our actions carefully before we implement them. For example, if on reflection we suspect that our actions could in any way bring pain and misery to someone else, we need to avoid them at all cost. Giving up any such thought immediately is crucial, because if we were to act on the thought, we would build negative karma for our own selves. When we stop, consider, and consult our higher minds, the conscious choices that we make as a result have unlimited positive potential. They open the way for us to generate and to benefit from two greatest powers of the human soul—the power of goodness and the power of kindness.

The Power of Goodness

We are creations of God and his goodness exists in our souls. There is thus no higher power within us. Goodness has no substitutes, and it cannot be faked. Goodness springs from our hearts and spirits. It is a quality that we bring with us when we are born, and which we have acquired over lifetimes as a soul. Each soul remembers the good within itself and also knows what its weaknesses are, for improving these is the reason the soul has taken birth on Earth.

Spirituality and improvement go hand in hand. If we improve, we rise spiritually and if we backslide, we degrade the spirit. It is a constant movement governed by our thoughts, words, and actions. The higher our spiritual values and the more we follow the good and godly spiritual path, the faster we will rise and the closer will be our connection with God and our higher minds. Through that connection, we activate the power of goodness within us.

Once activated, goodness empowers us to choose right over wrong, and our earthly choices therefore improve. We are less likely to succumb to the temptations of greed, success, wealth, power, and politics. We are more likely to seek out the ongoing peace and happiness that comes from selfless service to others. With better choices and the improve actions that follow, we rise in consciousness and our souls grow spiritually. We thus become part of a positive cycle in which we move all the closer to God and become ever more able to generate and grow through the power of goodness.

Life is a journey to be enjoyed while it lasts. We can struggle to capture and to cling to the fleeting happiness associated with materialism and selfish choices. Or we can savour meaningful lives empowered by goodness. The choice is always ours.

The Power of Kindness
Kindness is a feeling of goodwill that comes from within and manifests as any helpful act that one human being bestows on another. Such acts come in many forms. What they all have in common is that each one is important to another human being. No kind act is too big or too small. What matters is the positive impact that it has on another person's life. How does an act of kindness change the other person's view of the world or of another human being? One act might not change the world or even a measurable fraction of the population, but if it touches one soul on Earth and that person starts regarding life and other human beings in a positive way, something important has been accomplished.

We are often too busy in our day-to-day schedule to take a moment to even listen to another person's cry for help. We see depression and unhappiness in people and the environment. We see dampened spirits and unhappy faces, but we neglect to ask a simple question: What is bothering you and how can I be of help? Just listening to someone else's problems in life is a kindness that can go a long way. One young man, Joe, learned this from his workplace mentor:

Nathan was a manager in a financial Institution. Joe had joined Nathan's team to gain work experience and to earn money to complete his undergraduate degree. Joe considered Nathan to be his mentor and they got along well. After his summer position ended, Joe moved to another department, but he kept in touch with Nathan and occasionally sought his guidance. Nathan could relate to the younger man, because he had a son who was Joe's age.

One day, Joe came to Nathan to seek his advice, as he had an opportunity to join a small start-up company. Nathan listened and advised Joe to stay in his current position. In the course of the discussion he asked Joe if he had discussed his current career options with his parents. Joe confided that he could not connect much with his dad, who had a different philosophy in life and was, at times, difficult to reason with. Because of the constant tension between his father and himself, Joe was estranged from his family. This rift went back two years, during which time the father's health had deteriorated to the point that he had been forced to shut down his business.

Nathan chose his words carefully. Without trying to make Joe feel guilty, he tactfully suggested the possible connection between Joe's separation from the family and his dad's loss of health. The father's suffering might in part arise from the unresolved differences between himself and Joe. Nathan pointed out that Joe's dad was born and raised in a different culture and thus had different perceptions from Joe's. But that did not mean that he loved Joe any less.

Joe saw the connection. Something resonated in his heart as he left Nathan's office. This was during the Christmas season, and three days later, Nathan found a card from Joe on his desk. It read: "Best boss to work with. Only a father would know the pain that another father is going through." Joe reconnected with his dad and mom during the Christmas holiday and continued to maintain the relationship on a weekly basis. Joe and Nathan stayed in touch with one another, although both of them ended up working for different organizations.

This story is a perfect example of how one kind act of listening and relating to another can have wide ramifications. Joe took Nathan's advice and did not accept the job with the small company; he later moved on to a better job. Joe also took to heart Nathan's considered comments about his differences with his dad and re-established their relationship. Even though Nathan did not know Joe's dad, he was still able to empathize with him through Joe. This is an instance of how we are all connected and will continue to stay connected because we all originate from the same Creator.

To be truly kind, an act has to spring from the heart and be pure and untainted in intention. We should not be looking for fame and glory by helping someone. On the contrary, we want to be silent workers, touching someone's heart and then moving toward our next destination in the journey of spreading kindness.

The 2014 Sochi Olympics produced lots of stories. One of the most exhilarating and selfless of them captured the hearts of all Canadians, including mine, and inspired people of other nations as well: Gilmore Junio, a Canadian speed skater, voluntarily gave up his spot in the 1000-metre event, so that Denny Morrison, his colleague, friend, and teammate could compete. Gilmore relinquished his spot, knowing Denny stood a better chance and, sure enough, Denny proved himself by winning the silver medal for Canada. Through Gilmore's act, kindness flowed from himself to Denny and inspired millions in their own lives.

Another kind of situation, drawn from my own experience, happened in 1995, in Mumbai, India. My son was two years old and he was sick. The fever was not going down and the medicine was not having any effect. I called the pediatrician and he told me to bring my son to his clinic. We took a cab and, in the middle of our journey, there was a police barricade and no traffic was allowed through, due to violence and disturbances in the neighbouring area. I learned that a curfew was in effect and included the zone in which the pediatrician's clinic was located.

I approached a constable and pled my case. He looked at my son and realized the seriousness of his condition. He said that he had a son of the same age and knew how helpless a parent feels in such a situation. He told the other constables that he was proceeding on official escort duty, started his motor bike, and directed the taxi driver to follow him. At each barrier he stated that we were with him, and the taxi was waved through. I couldn't thank him enough when we reached the clinic.

The pediatrician was waiting for us, checked my son, and prescribed new medication. When we returned to the waiting cab, the police constable was still there too. He escorted us back to the safe area and, when we reached our destination, I thanked him for his kind deed. He told me, "God gave me an opportunity to do something better in life today."

On our drive back home, I thought to myself, *God works in mysterious ways*, and I thanked him for sending the help when I needed it most. As I was having these thoughts, the taxi driver commented that he had never in all his years of driving seen a police constable going so far beyond the line of duty to help someone. This incident was moving and unforgettable for me. I learnt the important lesson that we don't need to know someone to help someone. If we have the will to kindness, God will use us as instruments to serve others in life.

A person will only appreciate kindness after going through a life-learning incident such as I experienced that night in Mumbai. Such acts of kindness are never forgotten. They stay embedded in our souls and spirits. An act of kindness is part of a chain that never ends. One person helps another, and the one helped goes on to be kind to someone else, and so on and on . . . There are no barriers to kindness. Race, culture, ethnic background, nationality, religion, and gender are irrelevant because kindness arises from a soul level and passes from soul to soul. The soul knows to provide kindness at the right moment to anyone that might need it. And so the links in the chain multiply.

Never hesitate, therefore, to be kind. Doing an act of kindness is like pumping lifeblood into another human being. Ultimately, we will be measured by the selfless deeds and kindnesses that we have performed with pure motives. We all need help and support in life. What better way to encourage another person on their spiritual journey than with an act of kindness?

• • •

Inspirational Connections

- Power is a gift from God, to be used wisely.
- Earthly, or external, power, can be used negatively to satisfy your ego; or it can be used positively to make a difference in others' lives through sharing and serving.
- Avoid abuse of power by making positive, conscious choices; practise meditation to connect with your higher mind.
- Your inner power is linked to your higher mind and, through that, to your spiritual consciousness.
- Your inner power includes free will: you can choose to raise or to lower your consciousness, to be happy or miserable.
- Through the conscious exercise of your free will, you open the way to creating and experiencing the powers of goodness and kindness; thus you move closer to God.

9
Spiritual Truths and Individual Truth

It is not possible to arrive at Truth and ignore consciousness, because Truth is the very product of consciousness.

—David R. Hawkins, M.D., Ph.D.

IN ORDER TO FULFILL our lives, we need to understand and accept the basic spiritual truths. These truths provide direction and set us on the spiritual path. We are born knowing certain spiritual truths, but our materialistic, high-tech world tends to draw us toward technology, materialistic wealth, success, fame, glory, and glamour—to the extent that many have forgotten the spiritual truths that are embedded in our souls.

There are many spiritual truths, of which the most essential are the following:

1. There is only one God, who is divine, supreme, all powerful and Creator of all universes.
2. We are the creations of God, and the energy that resides in each human being is a spark of energy from God.
3. God has provided each of us with a higher mind and a conscience.
4. We each have a physical body, a physical mind, a soul, and a higher mind.
5. We are spiritual beings having an earthly experience to advance and refine our souls.
6. The higher mind is the guiding force and greatest asset of each one of us.
7. We all have free will to make conscious choices on Earth.
8. Each individual's Earth journey is unique, and each individual possesses a different level of consciousness.

An understanding of the great spiritual truths is the foundation for raising our consciousness. If our grasp of these truths is not firm, we will always be confused, and our physical minds will be in constant struggle with our higher minds. The physical mind will at times deny the existence of God, higher power, soul awareness, and all that is spiritual, whereas the higher mind always wants each of us to expand our knowledge—in particular, to gain wisdom and insight about God and God's creations—so that we can raise our awareness and lead conscious lives on Earth.

Awareness and Spiritual Truths
Awareness of the spiritual truths develops in various stages, and it begins when we are ready and willing to listen to our higher minds. Awareness increases when we are open to acknowledging the spiritual truths, when we are not fighting them logically with our physical minds, when we are not trying to find excuses to disbelieve them, and when we stop trying to prove that spiritual truths do not exist. This kind of awareness is linked to our own consciousness. The higher our consciousness, the less resistance we will have to accepting the spiritual truths and leading godly, good lives on Earth—lives that we build around spiritual faith. We accept and embrace these spiritual truths as part and parcel of our earthly journeys; we need to embrace the spiritual truths and to integrate each and every one into all facets of our lives.

Although our physical minds might try to obscure and complicate them, the spiritual truths are plain and simple. We can accept them willingly at an early or a later stage in life. Or we can have complete disbelief throughout our lives, but we will have to accept these truths once we complete our earthly journeys and move back to the spirit world. Once we land in the spirit world, we will realize that we did not invest our time wisely on Earth. We will realize that we wasted our lives by not following the path, by not listening to our higher selves, and by not following God's path and purpose. We were born on Earth for spiritual improvement but we wasted it on something else. We were drawn toward materialistic wealth, greed, dishonesty, and other negative qualities—the very temptations that we were born on Earth to overcome but which we succumbed to yet again. We need to understand that our greatest "investment" on Earth is in our soul journey.

When we lack awareness we are in a dream. One fine day we wake up and realize that what we have been doing all our lives was wrong. We were following the wrong path and now want to get out of that nasty dream and move toward God's light. We see purpose in our lives. We see God's plan and existence in every step of the way and start feeling that the journey on Earth has meaning after all. We were all meant to lead godly, good lives, to be of assistance to others, to overcome our negative soul characteristics, and to find a role in the universe that will bring peace to each of us on Earth.

When we get that feeling, we are each aligned with our own spirit. We therefore want to lead lives that serve others and put us at peace with others on Earth. God has given us this earthly opportunity to improve, and we need to use it wisely, to rise in awareness, to do what we feel is right, and not to worry about what others think of us. We need to act with goodness in our hearts, and the universe will return the goodness to us in one form or another. We need to be at peace, and then peace will follow us wherever we go. We need to be humble, and humility will meet us at our doorsteps. We need to be loving, and we will be loved in all our relationships. We need to be driven and work toward God's cause and purpose, and all will be well for us in our lives.

Understanding Truth

Once we accept the spiritual truths, we open the doors to the purpose for our existence on Earth—our divine mission to learn, grow, and evolve our souls. We come to realize that life has greater meaning than the petty concerns of the daily routine. Our souls are channelled to listening to our higher minds all the time, and the higher mind guides us toward becoming our true selves and leading sincere and truthful lives on Earth. Knowing with conviction that our earthly journeys have meaning, we start to believe that leading truthful lives is important, and that the only way to lead such a life is to be a model of it, by always speaking the truth and acting faithfully upon it.

Each individual has the choice to accept and champion the spiritual truths that will help all of us progress on our earthly journeys. Some individuals have abundant knowledge about spirituality but are afraid to even voice their opinions, let alone to actively guide someone toward the spiritual path. The basic factor that inhibits many human beings is fear of adverse reactions: Will the other person be put off by my beliefs? What if I were to lose my friendship? What if I am faced with other unpleasant consequences?

Such concerns are unnecessary. For upholding the spiritual truths brings clarity to all illusions, misconceptions, and false perceptions that we might have in our lives. We are all searching for truth from our friends, families, colleagues, and others in the universe. But, above all, we must also search for the most important truth of all—the truth that lies within each of us, and which is integral to our leading purposeful lives. The truth within each of us is the light that emanates from the conscience, showing us right action, and illuminating the path of positivity and peace.

Components and Levels of Truth

Truth has two components: the speaker who wants to convey the truth and the listener who is interested and willing to listen to truth. Truth can only be conveyed if the speaker has the courage, humility, and confidence to convey the truth without any fear of repercussions, such as losing a friendship or relationship, and the listener has the humility to listen to the truth with clear conscience and fair judgment to respect what is being said.

In spiritual terms, the speaker is the higher mind and the listener is the physical mind. The higher mind always guides us toward truth and prompts us to lead an honest and a sincere life on Earth. The physical mind has the power either to accept and implement what comes from the higher mind or to disregard the voice of the higher mind and perform acts that are not in the best interest of our souls and spirits. The role of the higher mind is to continuously guide us toward truth, light, and God's path. But if we keep on ignoring the advice of the higher mind, it will become silent after a certain period of time. It is in this particular phase of silence that we start making wrong choices, because we have disconnected ourselves from the higher mind and can no longer benefit from its guidance in our day-to-day lives. Once we start making unconscious choices, it becomes a habit. We decline in spiritual awareness, our spirits degrade instead of evolving, and we are increasingly drawn to selfishness, greed, and actions that lack the presence of God. When we allow our spiritual consciousness to decline to such a low level, we inevitably continue to make unconscious choices in life—it is a negative, self-perpetuating cycle.

All is not lost, however, if we really want to take the path to God, his light, and his purpose. A genuine desire to change and to move toward spiritual consciousness is the first step, and we need to reinforce it with sincere and heartfelt prayers. If we start with these basic steps—a willingness to change and a commitment to prayer—our higher minds will once again show us the right direction in all aspects of life.

Spiritual Truth, Wellness, and Authenticity
On the spiritual level, each individual needs to tap into the truth that is the essence of his or her genuine, or higher self. We need to acknowledge the fact that, in each of us, there is a deep connection of body, mind, and spirit. How we each lead life on Earth impacts our own spirit, which means that we can never really separate our physical actions and thoughts from our own individual truth. We might delude ourselves that such a separation is possible, but the end result of doing so is not only spiritual regression but often bodily and emotional malaise as well. If, on the other hand, we are true and attentive to our higher selves, and act according to this individual spiritual truth, then we will feel physically and mentally fit—healthy, rejuvenated, content, and peaceful in life.

In the spiritual dimension of our lives, we must always put our faith and trust in God. Such unconditional trust is the link between us and the Creator, and it is so powerful that it allows us to weather the darkest of life's storms, hurdle every obstacle, and meet all of life's challenging experiences with confidence and positivity.

When we do not seek our own spiritual truth, we cannot be happy inside. However enviable might be our external, earthly situations, our spiritual emptiness renders life meaningless and lacklustre. Prestigious jobs lose their charm; seemingly ideal relationships with our children, spouses, families, and friends are in fact devoid of honesty. Though we might try to silence it, a small inner voice tells us that we are fakes and hypocrites. And, indeed, how can we be authentic if we ignore our higher selves and the spiritual truth within each of us?

Intentions That Define Truth

When we seek or speak the truth, the intention behind the deeds and words is very important. Are we trying to discover or convey a higher truth that will be beneficial to another person? Or are we using brutal honesty disguised as truth in order to create pain and misery for someone else? These are questions well worth asking ourselves, for every intention has its consequences. When truth is abused out of self-interest, the consequences will always be negative. While we may elude a bad outcome in earthly life, we disappoint our higher selves and add to our karmic debt.

If our motives are peaceful and benign, if we are genuinely trying to benefit another person, then we are delivering truth from a soul level. If our intention is to cause pain and misery to the other person, we are delivering it from a negative place in our hearts. When we thus discard the voice of the higher mind and listen to the egotism of the physical mind, we are not delivering truth.

There is a vast difference between a factual, or true, statement and a spiritual truth. The factual statement is typically straightforward and verifiable. Depending on the intention behind it, a statement of fact might, on the one hand, cause pain and unhappiness or, on the other, relief and happiness. Spiritual truth, however, has only kind of effect—positive—because it comes from soul level, and our souls never promote the idea of harming anyone, intentionally or unintentionally. Spiritual truth always draws us toward light and peace, toward sharing and caring for every human being on the planet. It does not have a specific hidden agenda to satisfy the ego. It has a specific mission, and that mission is to bring peace, love, harmony, and happiness into the universe.

The Journey toward Spiritual Truth
The path of spiritual truth is not easy to follow, but the way becomes smoother each time we listen to our higher minds and follow the basic spiritual truths. Among the most important of these truths are believing in God, fulfilling life's purpose, helping others, and heightening our individual spiritual awareness. Each time we listen to our higher minds, we implement these truths. When we integrate these truths in our lives, we enjoy a sense of inner peace. We feel closer to our friends, family, and employees. Above all, we are connected to our higher selves and the spirit within each of us, which in turn helps us lead our lives consciously.

An individual's life is his or her own journey. We can consciously choose to lead our lives with lies, or with truth. When we don't speak the truth, we create a lot of mental and emotional frustration in our minds, because we have not released the negative energy that we cling to with our physical selves. We seem to have the same thoughts over and over again in our physical minds—which does not allow us to move forward in life.

Bottling up the truth inside ourselves also has a negative impact on our physical bodies. The more we suppress the truth and lack the courage to express it, the more that we are likely to suffer from medical and physical problems. There are times when our circumstances do not allow us to speak the truth; for example, we value our job so much that we hesitate to speak up about wrongdoing in the organization or department. Such a situation illustrates that espousing the ideal of truth is a choice that is easy to make but often difficult to implement. When we find ourselves in a dilemma, we must strive to remember that each soul longs to speak the truth, to know the truth, and to share the truth, because the benefits of truth far exceed the benefits of not speaking the truth. It is also our spiritual duty toward our souls to seek, to uphold, and to speak the truth.

Truth needs to be recognized. It needs to be uncovered and made apparent to others. When the truth is revealed, the recipient changes his or her perception of life and of others on Earth. Truth—in both its revelation and reception—is pure light; it is wisdom with no conditions attached. Truth trails justice and clarity in its wake. It quiets nagging doubts and puts the troubled past behind us. Truth reclaims lost souls and repairs broken relationships. Most of all, truth promotes forgiveness and helps us move forward freely in our life journeys on Earth. And we do so with the inner satisfaction that, in championing truth, we have not only benefited ourselves and other human beings but also contributed to the peace and kindness in the universe.

. . .

Inspirational Connections

- You are born with soul knowledge of spiritual truths.
- These eternal spiritual truths lead to the spiritual truth within you as an individual.
- The truth within you lights the way to positivity and peace.
- Even if you feel that you have lost your own truth, a sincere desire to change will lead you back to it.
- Spiritual truth is always positive and beneficial because it comes from soul level.
- Truth needs to be recognized and revealed—it is your spiritual duty to do so.
- Truth reclaims lost souls and repairs broken relationships.
- Thus you move forward with the inner satisfaction that comes from fulfilling your purpose in life and the universe.

10
Life and the Benefits of Purposeful Living

Happiness cannot be traveled to, owned, earned, worn, or consumed. Happiness is the spiritual experience of living every minute with love, grace, and gratitude.

—Denis Waitley

WE CAN ONLY UNDERSTAND the significance of human life if we believe that we are born on Earth for a purpose. Each of our lives has a specific meaning and our souls are eternal. We take birth and rebirth, and we reincarnate in different human forms. We choose our existence on Earth so that we can fulfill our mission on Earth, which is to improve spiritually, evolve, and align with God's plan for the universe.

Our lives on Earth allow our souls to progress or regress. Either way, life does not just happen to any of us. We shape our lives mainly through our actions. In the same way, we also create the destiny of our souls, for our actions are ultimately translated into karma. To understand life, and to lead it wisely, we must always be mindful of the spiritual truths that shine the light by which we navigate a fulfilling journey on Earth.

If this sounds like a daunting commitment, take heart, for there are basic strategies that we can readily implement in our daily lives, and thus stay in accord with the spiritual truths. These strategies, which come from the soul level, include welcoming life's possibilities, living in the present moment, practising forgiveness, valuing learning, curbing impulsiveness, avoiding greed and envy, and managing expectations. Putting these strategies into effect, even in small ways, not only ensures that we follow the path of purposeful living but also rewards us many times over in emotional and spiritual abundance.

Welcoming Life's Possibilities

Life is a blessing. We learn from each and every incident, interaction, and relationship with others. Life offers us spiritual growth and advancement. It also doles out some bumps and bruises along the way, so that we can learn and not repeat the same mistakes again. Life makes us wise, so that we can guide others, and most of all, life shows us the path of consciousness. It shows us how to face our challenges, to go through each day with a smile, and to heal ourselves and others by our actions. Most importantly, life provides us with opportunities to care, love, forgive, and be compassionate toward others.

What is surprising—even shocking—is that with all the abundance and opportunities that life offers, many people openly state that they do not like their lives. How can this be when, as souls, they chose to be reborn into a certain family, country, and environment? The answer is that they really don't like the way that they are currently leading their lives. They each feel their own soul's unhappiness because they have closed their minds and hearts to the opportunities that earthly existence presents to them every single day. In this way, the link between each soul and the Creator is either weakened or broken.

To ensure that we keep moving closer to God, we need to be open to all possibilities in life. Everything that happens to us has a reason. In our physical minds, we might have a rationale for thinking we should move in a particular direction. Meanwhile, for another greater reason, the universe is pulling us in another direction. The reason of the universe is final. It is always fruitful and in the best interest of everyone's needs, karma, and grace. All is fair from a universal point of view.

If we abandon our stubborn resistance and open our closed physical minds to what life holds for us, we will each be driven toward our purpose, our soul fulfillment, and what we were born to achieve on Earth. We will be guided toward work that will satisfy the needs of our souls. We will be pulled into projects that will nourish our minds and makes us happy. We each have a perfect spot in the universe and we will find the perfect job or role where our skills and talents will be utilized and where we will be able to contribute to the needs of the universe.

Because we are all born for a purpose and things happen for a reason, staying open to *all* of life's possibilities empowers each of us to make a difference on Earth. While the universe will always pull us in the right direction, it is nonetheless up to each of us to ensure that our own consciousness is active and at its peak. This happens when we continuously listen to our higher minds and follow the godly, good path. The higher our consciousness, the easier it will be to find our purpose on Earth. The higher our consciousness, the tougher will be our spiritual training and tests, but the greater will be our ability to overcome every challenge. Through facing life with openness and positivity we shift our individual consciousness and our energy moves toward God's energy, which has the single purpose of selflessly serving other souls on Earth.

Loving others is the first step. Removing hatred and animosity at all cost is the second step. Not judging people and accepting the way things are is the third step. If we integrate all three of these steps into our daily lives, we will each see a change in our own self and spirit. Not only will this change make us aware that our spirits are growing more refined and pure, but it will also attract the favourable notice of the people with whom we interact in our day-to-day lives.

Life offers us all the opportunities that are good for the soul and the spirit. It is we who make the choice to reject these opportunities and select things that give us passing mental and physical gratification. Our choices allow us to shape our own soul personalities. Our choices will either make us happy, loving, and pleasant, or they will make us unhappy, unloving, and miserable to be around. When we welcome life's opportunities we are most likely to restrain our physical minds, please our souls, and lead happy lives on Earth.

Living in the Present Moment
Life is full of surprises. If we walk on the godly, good path, life has more sweetness to offer us day by day, minute by minute. Cherish every moment, for when the moment is gone, it can never be relived. We must cherish the present and enjoy what comes our way.

At work, we function best when we focus on doing one thing at a time. We need to stop our physical minds from wandering here and there. With the energy thus rechanneled, we can put our bodies, minds, hearts, and souls into the effort required to complete the task at hand. Not only will this get the job done, but it will also eliminate the stress of procrastination and worries about meeting deadlines. Life—and our work in life—is meant to bring us mental peace and happiness, but this will not happen if we allow ourselves to be distracted by things that are not good for our own spirits.

These distractions might include indulging in activities that sidetrack us from our main work, pursuing goals that are detrimental to the spirit, and grasping at supposed opportunities that are really dead ends. Often we go in these unproductive directions because we are not thinking of the moment but, rather, are looking ahead to hoped-for prestige, power, and status. At best, succumbing to distractions wastes the present moment and, at worst, can directly or indirectly hurt others that we may let down, impede, or even betray as we pursue our own haphazard inclinations.

Outside of work, when we are dealing with loved ones and family situations, living peacefully in the present moment can be a great test of both our patience and our ingenuity as we endeavour to make every moment count. I had a friend whose wife was working different shifts and he would go to pick her up, especially during the night shift which would end at eight or nine o'clock in the evening. His wife's role was customer service and advising clients, and as a result, she would often get caught up in a situation and put in extra time at work. My friend, meanwhile, would be sitting in the parking lot outside her workplace, fuming about how her lateness was a waste of his time. This would happen most of the time when he went to pick her up, and every time, he would react when she came out late. The resulting argument would spoil the ride home and the rest of the night. Over time, this petty matter began to erode their entire relationship.

Tired of the arguing, my friend decided to change his attitude about the time he spent waiting for his wife. He made up his mind that no matter how long she took, he was not going to react. This might sound like a tense exercise of willpower but, in fact, it turned out to be a pleasurable experience. There were two activities my friend loved, and which he could do in a car, in a parking lot: reading good books and praying. He bought a good book and prayer beads and kept them in his glove compartment. Now, when he goes to pick up his wife, he sends a text—"waiting outside," and he will either read the book or pray. Even though he still has to wait for his wife each time he goes to pick her up, he has stopped reacting because he is focusing on the moment and investing his time in doing what he loves. He has stopped reacting to the extent that he no longer even asks her the reason for being late.

Living in the moment—savouring the moment—not only helps us let go of the past and quit worrying about a future that might not materialize. As my friend's story illustrates, living in the moment is an effective strategy for accepting many everyday situations with calmness. The more we do so, the better it is for the harmony of our workplaces and family relationships. Suppressing impatient or otherwise negative reactions repays karma. The more we practise this kind of restraint, the easier it gets and the purer we become in spirit. When we take charge of our reactions in this way, we should feel encouraged because each instance of forbearance is a sign to us that we are changing and shifting our own consciousness to a higher level.

Practising Forgiveness

As human beings with feelings, we often find it difficult not to be angry or vengeful when others have done something wrong that affects our own lives. Such responses often seem reasonable to us, but this is an illusion that arises from our being conditioned to the negative thoughts and feelings that run through our physical minds, day and night. We must therefore make a constant effort to empty our minds of anger, desire for revenge, and unforgivingness. Living in the moment is not just a way to stay calm, but it also helps foster forgivingness. When we stop harbouring anger from the past and revenge fantasies for the future, we are in a position to forgive.

When someone hurts us, forgiving moves us ahead into a better and more comfortable place, a place that is filled with peace and love. When we leave the negative feelings behind, we unburden ourselves, and our souls feel lighter. We have more energy, our physical minds are clearer, and our view of the world is in balance.

When we no longer have distorted perceptions, we are able to see that some of our negativity was the product of self-pity, a feeling that our physical minds often relish, but which does not work for our souls. Our souls always want to move past self-pity toward forgiveness. This is because our souls understand that the wrong done to us is part of God's plan for our spiritual growth and the refinement of our souls. We should therefore accept the incident and what life has offered us on Earth; we need to remember the experience but forget the hurt and the people that have inflicted it. We must forgive them, for that is how we move ahead in life and feel lighter in mind, heart, and spirit.

The more we forgive, the cleaner will be each of our spirits as we progressively give up our negative soul characteristics. The soul longs to be in a place of purity and pure thoughts. It does not want to be darkened by hatred, revenge, and the desire to humiliate others. What do we lose by letting go? The answer of course is *nothing*—on the contrary, we gain spiritual wisdom, purity of soul, and better mental and physical health. God wants us to practise forgiveness, for every time we do so, we move further along the path of purposeful living—and closer to the Divine presence.

Valuing Learning

Learning, of course, does not just come out of books. The kind of learning that supports purposeful living comes from our life experiences and the lessons we draw from them. Learning at this level enables us to see the bigger picture and grasp the meaning of our journeys on Earth. Every incident—good or bad, pleasant or unpleasant—has a deeper meaning for the soul. The potential for learning is everywhere—it is universal.

What we each learn as an individual may be very different from what someone else learns from the same experience. The principle, however, applies to everyone. We are students of life's school, and the lessons we learn are for the improvement of our souls.

Learning is part of God's plan to draw us nearer to him. Learning therefore never ends. If we open ourselves to it, we grow in wisdom and purity. We become able to understand the meaning of life, its purpose, and our own choices. Learning is the foundation for our soul's development. Once we have understood the lessons of our current lives, they stay embedded in our souls, and we carry the learning with us when we pass on to the spirit world. The cycle is continuous and we bring back our soul wisdom when we are reborn on Earth. Such learning not only benefits ourselves but also helps us connect with, and serve, other souls.

Curbing Impulsiveness

Learning goes hand in hand with thinking, and taking time to stop and think is often the way to diffuse a hostile encounter or to relax a tense situation. There is never any need to react hastily or negatively, for unconsidered or argumentative reactions do not help our souls. We must not be impulsive in our words and actions. It is always in our own best interests to think, and to think clearly, before we act and speak.

Life brings us a myriad of experiences. In any given situation, it is important to remain alert to the reactions of our bodies, physical minds, and hearts. Taking time to assess our feelings and possible responses is always helpful. If our emotions are often negative, and we reflect on the reason underlying them, we usually see a consistent pattern of triggers that fire our feelings and potentially cause us to react badly. Some triggers are petty and some are big—anything from the twitch of someone's lip to a barrage of insults. There are times when I can observe the negative triggers that affect me and actually feel the resultant emotions running through my mind and body. I can almost taste the negative words that I want to speak in order to hurt someone. But this is when the higher self intervenes and shows me the path of calmness and patience. In moments such as this, the higher self controls the physical mind to such an extent that the latter loses its ability to react. It becomes weak and compliant to the guidance of the higher mind. Every time I experience this, I am aware of both the weaknesses that reside in me and my own negative triggers. I have learned to use this awareness to help me to refine and purify my spirit in order to properly handle the next triggering moment in my life.

Our responsibility as individuals is to assess each situation and to judge how our actions and words are going to affect other people with whom we interact. This kind of careful, ongoing attention to the impact of our words and deeds is a fundamental strategy for easing the lives of other people and ourselves. We can be pleasant to others or we can be crude or rude. We can be kind or arrogant. The choices are always in our own hands. If we curb impulsive action and speech, and instead, with pure hearts, give thoughtful service to others, we will have good lives and a lessening of our own and others' pain and suffering on Earth.

Praying regularly not only helps us connect with God but also has a calming effect on the mind, so that we are less likely to act on impulse. The greater the amount of time that we dedicate to faithful prayer, the easier it gets to move thoughtfully through our lives.

Avoiding Greed and Envy

Each person's journey is different. Each journey has a unique aspect that is not relevant to any other person. Our own singular journey is based on our choices, our karma, and how we treat others in life—ideally with love, dignity, equality, and respect. As different as our journeys may be, they all ultimately have one purpose—to grow spiritually. And they have a single final destination—to arrive at oneness with God. At the soul level, therefore, there is no point to feeling greed or envy.

The earthly world, however, has a different agenda. It teaches us one main thing, which is to advance materially through power, attitude, position, and competition. The earthly world does not often encourage us to calmly face our problems and challenges. But if it were to do so, then the basic fear of what life is going to offer next would be eliminated. As things stand, we are always tense, worried and anxious. This is because we always feel the need to survive in the midst of all the greed, envy, jealousy, hatred, animosity, and unhealthy competition in this world. Many people's earthly life's mantra is to get things at any cost—to snatch status and wealth without restraint and to control others through the misuse of power and politics.

The world was not created for that. It was created to share, love, help, and serve, but we are so disjointed in mind, body, and spirit, and so often distanced from the Source that, at times, we hardly have an empathetic thought to share, or the will to stay connected to our Creator. Our life's journey was mapped out to be conducted at one level, but we are travelling at a different, lower level. Driven by greed and envy, many simply follow the crowd, hoping, or falsely believing, that this is the way to success and fulfillment. The exceptions are those who believe in a Higher Power and in fulfilling their individual life's purpose on Earth. Travelling the spiritual path is not easy but it can be done. Our souls know the path, and what we have to do is to control our physical minds so that we can receive the wisdom of our higher minds.

Greed and envy can be avoided when we learn to live in the following alternative states of being:

1. Contentment: True happiness lies in contentment. We must always be contented with the current situations in our lives, because God's timing and plan are perfect.
2. Purity: We feel God's presence in our hearts and souls. When we pray, our prayers should be short, sincere, and genuine, so that we make a direct connection with God.
3. Positivity: Even in the most difficult and lowest period of our lives, we should think positively in order to drive away greed and envy, and to create favourable outcomes in our lives.

Managing Expectations

Life takes us on a spiritual journey. Life provides opportunities for learning and evolution. Life allows us choices to expand our soul consciousness and to live in peace and harmony. Life presents abundant opportunities to follow the principles of God Almighty, to uphold spiritual truths, and to develop virtues. Life gives us every chance to fight the negativity that resides within us. Life offers us ways to make our souls pure, to serve the purpose of God, and to emerge victorious in spirit. Life enables us to be giving, loving, caring, honest, and truthful in all our relationships.

These are just some of life's meaningful gifts. And yet we humans often want more and could readily add our own long lists of grandiose expectations from life. We might demand that life give us a particular job, a substantial amount of money, and an impressive title with all the associated authority and power. In our private lives, we want a perfect partner, love, respect, and healthy relationships. Our struggles to realize our expectations can engage us in unhealthy competitions at work or within our own family circles as we maneuver to be seen as supreme, powerful, enviable, or even famous. More often than not, when we get what we expected, we are still not happy; and if we fail to have our expectations met, we can become depressed and disillusioned with life. When we mismanage our expectations and let them get out of hand, we are not flowing with what life is offering us at the current stage. And the flow is important because it brings balance to the body, mind, and spirit. It is the flow that generates peace and harmony in our souls, and when we have that, we experience joy and calmness in our lives. In the end, isn't that everything we could wish for?

Life is each soul's connection to Earth, other human beings, creatures, plants, and everything else. And all of us and all these things are connected to the Divine Source that is God. Sometimes, caught up in in our many earthly expectations, we neglect these all-important soul connections, and it takes an upset in life to set us straight.

Let us consider an example of someone who has lost his job due to restructuring. Before, his main focus was getting a promotion; now it is finding a job before the severance runs out. He might devote a few hours each day to searching and applying for jobs and to going for interviews. Even so, he now has time on his hands. This is a God-given opportunity for him to read good books, attend to his health, develop his fitness, and help others in the family by taking care of household chores.

There is thus a purpose in the loss of his job: the waiting period before resuming employment is an opportunity—a gift of time—for him to learn on a spiritual level. He starts to admire nature with more attention and finds that he has become more aware of all his surroundings, indoors and out. He notices that he has developed patience and is taking more time to react when someone throws angry words at him. He is now more likely than before to respond in a calm manner. Losing his employment prompted a sudden change in his lifestyle, and instead of resenting the change, he is turning it into a growth experience. In other words, he has taken a step toward accepting life and its outcomes, and is managing his expectations accordingly.

As this example suggests, life offers us what we require in any given moment of time. We therefore do not need to fight life, or to struggle for what it is not giving us, or to be unhappy with our circumstances. We simply need to trust in God and his universal powers. For we can have no greater expectation than the faith that all will be well in our lives, and that our journeys on Earth will be spiritually successful.

Sometimes, we let our earthly expectations soar so high that we become fearful of never attaining them. Hiding the fears, while desperately preserving the expectations, can cause us to act in ways that disdain others and disconnect us from our own souls. This reminds me of an employee who was working in sales department. His main responsibilities were to provide advice and to sell products. He was very smart and good at performing his job, but he was also very competitive, mean-spirited, rude, and arrogant. He was determined to achieve at any cost. He would manipulate clients and co-workers. No one could better him in any situation; any war of words always left him victorious. There was not a single person that he had not harmed or humiliated in the workplace in order to get what he wanted in life.

Life, however, shattered his expectations. One day, as he started his drive to work, his car skidded on a patch of black ice. He lost control of the car and injured himself badly. He was paralyzed from the waist down for few years before, fortunately, he eventually regained his normal health.

When we experience or hear about incidents like this, they give us cause for reflection. They are wake-up calls that remind us not to stray from the path of purposeful living and spiritual growth. For our earthly expectations can turn to nothing in a single moment, in the skid of a tire on ice, or in some other unforeseen mishap that can happen in an instant—and change our lives forever. How much more bearable such catastrophes would be if we had only nurtured our spirits instead of our expectations.

When we have too many expectations, and put too much stock in them, we can actually put our lives and our souls at risk. When life does not offer us what we need, we can feel hopeless, rejected, useless, and despondent. Have you ever lost hope with your own life? Have you valued or loved someone, or something, more in your life than your own life—and then lost that someone or something? Have you been ridiculed, humiliated, cheated, wronged, deprived, and run down day in and day out by someone in your life? Have you felt that you have not achieved anything and you are worth nothing? When feelings of hopelessness, worthlessness, and despair run through our heads, the power of our physical minds is so strong, so dominating and controlling, that we do not think from our higher minds. With our physical minds thus exaggerating our problems; we are all too likely to think of wrong solutions, which we believe are completely rational and true. One woman's tragic story illustrates how far being deluded by mismanaged expectations and wrong thinking can go:

Rani was in her early twenties when, with every expectation of living a prosperous and happy life, she married a prominent business man. Indeed, as she had anticipated, she received all the materialistic comforts that life could provide. There was never any shortage of money for spending on anything she wanted for herself, her family, and her friends. Despite all the wealth at her disposal, she was not happy because her husband was not faithful to her and was having an affair with another woman.

One day she found out that her husband, who had gone on a business trip, was accompanied by the same woman, and they took a vacation together. On finding this out, Rani felt totally helpless. Her whole life was falling to pieces—she was shattered from the inside out. She felt nothing was working in her life and would have traded all her wealth to receive the love and commitment she longed for from her husband. Although she had friends and family, she was too ashamed to divulge her marital situation to her family and to seek help from them. She believed that she had lost her battle with life and felt vulnerable, helpless, and manipulated. With hopelessness surrounding her day and night, Rani concluded that her existence had no meaning and that she did not matter in the universe. In this disordered state of mind, she drank a poisonous mix of chemicals that ended her life and left her family devastated.

Suicide, one of humanity's great tragedies, is an extreme example of allowing expectations to dictate actions. When faced with anguish and betrayal, most people manage to stop short of this final desperate measure. Even so, Rani's story carries a warning for us all: we must guard against confusing ourselves—our souls—with our expectations. When we fall into this trap, we are vulnerable to negative feelings, because we are trying too hard to control our lives and their outcomes. We are clinging too fiercely to expectations that life should unfold in a certain way.

In fact, life is like playing a game of sports. If we are angry, irritable, full of frustration, and determined to control the game, we will never be able to play it effectively. Similarly, in everything we undertake, we have to be calm and patient and do our best to flow with life. We as individuals can control our own actions but we cannot control someone else's actions. If things are not working out for us in life, we need to have the courage to move away and distance ourselves from the people and environments that are causing our grief and unhappiness.

When we allow our expectations to define us, our lives and our souls are in potential danger. If we fail to control a situation or a person to the satisfaction of our expectations, we are all too vulnerable to falling into a negative state of mind. If this state extends to the extremes of despair, then we lose our connection with our own soul. When this happens, we cease to value our own life and our reason for being born on Earth. Suicide thus becomes a possibility. If it escalates to a reality, then the tragedy is twofold. For the individual has not only lost his or her earthly life but has also fallen low spiritually. The negative karma that is accumulated as a result necessitates that the individual take a rebirth and repeat the same earthly training and tests all over again. To eliminate the earthly tragedy of suicide, and to avoid a constant cycle of rebirths, what we all need to remember is this: life is beautiful if you accept what comes your way and do not try to resist it. Life is also an adventure, for we cannot predict what it will reveal to us the next day or even the next moment. There is a vast difference between expectation and reality. If we could grasp this simple point, then when our own expectations are not met, we would not despair and become disaffected from life.

We are too much conditioned by our worldly perspective that we need to have certain things—good looks, money, material possessions, power, and status. In fact, beyond our basic comfort and security, we have no need for any of this. We only need to realize that we are already special, simply for who we are. Nothing can change that. The only thing that we can alter is our spiritual understanding, and once we change from the inside and let our spirits glow, the exterior world and its trappings of things and power will have no value and lose their charm.

When we do not realize some earthly expectation, it does not mean that life is cruel to us. It means that there is a better future without the thing or position or relationship that we have lost. We need to understand that the real significance of our so-called loss is that we are now better able to achieve our purpose in life. Had the expected outcomes materialized, our souls would not have progressed in the ensuing environment or state of mind. In other words, things happen for a reason. To grasp this basic soul knowledge and to put expectations in their place is to discover peace of mind, and something else: that much-desired feeling and ideal that many people find all too elusive these days—happiness.

Soul Strategies and the Benefits of Purposeful Living
Openness to life's possibilities. Living in the Moment. Forgiveness. Impulse control. Avoidance of greed and envy. Managing expectations. Incorporating these strategies, which come from soul level, into our daily lives will ensure that we continue to grow spiritually as we proceed on our earthly journeys. Knowing that we are thus being true to life's purpose is reward enough in itself. But this knowledge brings with it the added emotional benefits of peace of mind, satisfaction with life, and happiness. Finally, above all else—beyond all else—through purposeful living we stay constantly connected to our own souls, and thus to God.

• • •

Inspirational Connections

- A life of purposeful living is a life dedicated to the purpose of spiritual growth.
- You grow in spirit by knowing and upholding spiritual truths.
- To help you, your soul has strategies that you can incorporate into your daily life.
- These soul strategies are: (1) openness to life's potential; (2) savouring the present; (3) forgiving others; (4) continuously learning from life; (5) impulse control; (6) avoidance of negative states of mind, such as greed and envy; and (7) restraining soul-damaging expectations and accepting life as it unfolds.
- Purposeful living benefits you emotionally by enhancing your peace of mind, contentment with life, and personal happiness.
- Purposeful living benefits you spiritually by ensuring that you are always connected to your own soul.

11
Coping with Life's Challenges

*Life is a song—sing it. Life is a game—
play it. Life is a challenge—meet it.
Life is a dream—realize it. Life is a
sacrifice—offer it. Life is love—enjoy it.*

—Sai Baba of Shirdi

FAITH, TRUST, AND SURRENDER are the three guiding principles that we need to adopt in order to move ahead in life. We should never doubt the existence of God. Our spirits should have faith in God, trust the verdict of God, and surrender to God when we are faced with temptations and negative situations in life. If we pray and surrender, we get divine help and strength to make the right choices and to overcome the obstacles in our paths. When we surrender ourselves to

God, we are surrendering our problems to God. We lay our troubles at his feet and ask that he do what is best for us.

To surrender to God is to take the first step forward in life. The second step is to accept whatever life offers us. The solution to our problems that we are seeking from the universe will not be the solution offered to us. God's solution will be entirely different from what we anticipate, and we need to learn to accept it, for that is the wisdom in surrendering our problems and selves to God. The solution might not look attractive from our limited perspective, but it has a hidden meaning for our spiritual growth and development.

The more we learn to trust God and to surrender to him, the more we flow with life, and the more life flows with us. We are not in a struggle. We are at peace with ourselves and the universe. We do not question why things are happening to us in life but, rather, accept them as part of God's plan. For we know that God wants our own soul progression and development to contribute to the universe. Thus we do what is needed to meet life's challenges. We hold to faith—in people and in God; we practise patience; we act out of love; with pure intentions, we help others; and thus we partake wisely of the gift of life. Finally, we become all the more sure of coping purposefully with life's challenges when we cultivate gratitude; for grateful people do not just accept the principles of faith, trust, and surrender—they live them.

Faith

At some time in life, every person born on Earth puts his or her faith in someone else. A child puts his faith in his mother, father, and grandparents; and the parents trust that their children will all walk on the godly, good path. Teachers put their faith in students to learn and grow; and students look to their teachers to show them the right path to education, learning, training, and development. Ideally, employees have faith in their leaders and organization; and the organization entrusts its leaders and employees with performing their best for the whole. Without faith we would not be able to function as human beings and souls. We would be living in constant fear that others would cause us harm. Faith helps us bond, open up, share our problems, and listen to the advice and guidance that is provided by the person in whom we have faithfully confided. Faith goes hand in hand with trustworthiness, truth, honesty, and integrity. When other people live up to standards of integrity and display consistent values in all situations, our faith in them deepens, the bond between us and them strengthens, and the relationship flourishes at a soul level.

Compared to having faith in a Higher Power, putting faith in humans is easier to rationalize, because we can physically observe a consistent pattern of trustworthiness, strong values, honesty, and integrity. The faith that we place in our Creator, God Almighty, is of a higher order; it is intangible and not amenable to measurement and analysis. Depending on our individual soul development, we each either have faith in God, or we don't. When we have faith in our Creator, we accept what comes our way. We do not see problems as obstacles but as life's learning experiences or challenges, designed in order for the soul to evolve spiritually.

Faith begins with believing in God's existence. Faith then develops within our own souls and spirits. Faith grows when we elevate our soul consciousness and continuously accept each and every event of our lives as part of God's plan. Faith helps us change our mental perceptions, understand our soul development, and weather the toughest of times when no one is willing to help us and the doors of earthly justice are closed in our faces. When we are victims of harassment and abuse on Earth, it is our faith that keeps us going. Faith reduces stress, relieves mental anxiety, and creates peace in our bodies, minds, and spirits. This peace is available to all of us, as long as we are not too carried away with materialistic values and unrestrained expectations. We need only remember to have faith in God and to let life move us in the direction of God's plan, and not the plan that we want and think we deserve.

    Have faith and all will be well in life. Have faith and the Divine Lord will guide us in the right direction to help and serve others, and thus to fulfill our mission on Earth. Have faith, for there is nothing more powerful than faith in God. We need to have faith in our circumstances and to trust that all can, and will, change for the betterment of our souls. Our faith keeps us strong and makes us stronger; it helps us face life's challenges with peacefulness and calmness. Faith is that part of our souls that does not doubt the existence of God and a divine plan. Faith is the quality of a soul that believes that whatever happens is for our own spiritual growth, and that we will emerge successfully out of this experience. Faith is our love for God and our unconditional gratitude for this life and the opportunity to improve spiritually.

    Do not give up on faith. When we combine faith and love, we will be happy in whatever we do and say. Faith is our spiritual friend and partner when no other friend seems to stand by us in times of distress. Faith is the moment we believe in God no matter what the outcome is. Faith is the strengthening of our souls to such an extent that nothing can create doubts in our physical minds about the existence of God. Faith is life and meaningful life is faith. Faith moves us in fulfilling directions and we thus find the way to lead spiritual lives. Having faith—total, complete, positive and absolute—will make us stronger in spirit. It is our faith that will drive us to our spiritual destination. It is our faith that will heal our bodies, minds, and spirits.

Faith is connected to each of our souls and to all of the soul qualities that make us unique individuals. But while we all are different, we can each cultivate the willingness to progress in faith throughout our lifetimes. Faith can be renewed and increased by regular prayers and meditation. Faith can be expressed and sustained at all times in our daily routine if we love one another and generate goodwill and peace with our presence. It never hurts to smile more often and to make other people feel loved and cared for in this universe. Above all, we can always benefit by striving to be more generous and compassionate in all of our actions, and to let our feelings flow from the heart.

Whatever we do in our day-to-day existence, we must keep our faith strong. To falter in faith is to be negative and to erode the spirit. No matter what choices we make in life, we have to be sure that the spirit in each of us triumphs over the physical mind and what it tells us to do. If we keep faith, and flow with the spirit within each of us, it will never let us down and we will be assured of coping effectively with life's challenges.

Faith is the bridge between God and ourselves. Through faith, therefore, we know that all outcomes in life will be positive. So why waste energy by worrying? All our fears and anxieties change nothing. Everything will flow in the right direction according to God's plan and the laws of the universe.

God knows what is best for us and for our consciousness. Although our individual roles in God's plan may seem insignificant, in fact they have an impact. Each of us participates in the collective consciousness, and what we do, think, and say has a meaning for the universe. We each have the choice of raising or lowering our own consciousness; we need to choose wisely—for ourselves and for every other soul with whom we share this universe. Faith is the way.

Our faith gives us strength, makes us see the light, and helps us distinguish between right and wrong. Faith helps us go through our spiritual training and tests with ease; it is the shield that protects us from those that would harm us. Faith helps us overcome our fears and gives us the courage to face all our problems on Earth. In an imperfect world, faith is what keeps us going.

Patience

The test of patience is tough, but fortunately for us, having patience is interrelated with having faith in God. When we put our complete trust in the Almighty, we are strengthened, and with strength comes all the patience necessary to deal with our problems—whether they are caused by difficult people or troubling situations.

Times of stress and disappointment are when we are most likely to let our negative characteristics control our behaviour. It is often seems easier to get angry or irritable instead of taking reasonable action and then waiting patiently for the outcome. Cultivating patience can feel nearly impossible when our physical minds are screaming at us to do something—anything—to alleviate the current anxiety or discomfort. In such circumstances, it is helpful to remember that God has a plan, and it is based on the needs of the universe and of all the souls, including ourselves, who are struggling on Earth.

Let us take the classic example of a person who is technically qualified and has extensive work experience but is unable to find a job. Is this just bad luck, or could it be a test of patience?

Tom was an ambitious man with a wife and family to support. He was devastated when he was made redundant, and even a reasonable severance package did little to relieve his hurt pride and anxiety about the future of his career. Tom was a man of faith, but unemployment had focused all his attention on job searches and résumé writing. His normal practice of daily meditating fell by the wayside as he rose early and retired late, feverishly working at his computer and sending out application letters. His efforts paid off, and he went to several interviews. Each time, he would put on his best work clothes, square his shoulders, and fix a smile on his face. He wanted a job so badly that he was prepared to go to any limits to see that he got back on his chosen career path. But after each interview, he would soon find out that he had been passed over in favour of another candidate.

"What's wrong with me?" he asked his wife when he had received the latest rejection. She pointed out that he was well qualified and, thinking practically, suggested that he quit worrying for now, as he still had a few months of severance pay remaining. Being reminded that the situation was not entirely desperate had a calming effect on Tom. He became more selective in his job applications, put in less time at the computer, and resumed his practice of meditating. With meditation, he gained patience and was now prepared to wait for the right position to come along. He took comfort in realizing that while he wanted a job, he did not yet need one.

When another interview was in the process, Tom had a refreshed perspective—he would do his best as always, but this time he would calmly accept the result. So much had his attitude changed, that when he was offered the job at the end of the interview, he was gratified but hardly even surprised.

The universe tries to find a balance between a need and a want. As time passed and the employment that Tom wanted came closer to being what he truly needed, he was able to handle an interview in a way that got him a job offer. But there was more to his situation than just that. For a while, Tom had forgotten something crucial that he eventually remembered when he calmed down enough to return to his meditating. Problems, such as unemployment, help us evolve spiritually; they stimulate our souls to perform better and steer our inner spirits in the right direction. When we see life's challenges in this light, meeting them is as natural as landing a job eventually became to Tom. And all it took was a small amount of the patience that comes with faith.

Love

"Follow your heart," we often say—by which we mean: don't overthink; act out of love. Love is essential for each soul. Until we learn to love one another, we cannot progress to spiritual perfection.

Love is the ultimate spiritual learning, and it is a blessing to love, and to be loved by, someone. When we love, we show our caring, compassion, and kindness. When we love, we ignite a responsive spark in each of the people that receive our love. Our soul connection to others helps us continue to love them throughout earthly life. When we develop and sustain the ability to love others, we can never go wrong in our progress along the spiritual path.

Love is the ultimate soul characteristic. If we develop love toward others, all other positive soul characteristics are easier to achieve. With love we can exercise patience and conquer anger, hatred, jealousy, and vengefulness. With love we can heal suffering and overcome all the hardships that we might face in life.

The bonds of love last even after we die. This is because the soul lives on and retains all its characteristics when it passes from Earth to the spirit world. These characteristics that are embedded in our souls get rejuvenated or reignited when we take a rebirth. When we genuinely love others during our earthly lives, we come to recognize their true soul characteristics. Loving at this level in turn inspires the recipients to be loving toward others on Earth. In this way, love multiplies and it shifts both individual and collective consciousness to a higher level, thus making all of us better able to accept and deal with whatever obstacles life might throw in our paths.

Helping Others

We all cope the most effectively with life's challenges when we have the help of God, our friends, families, colleagues, and every person with whom we are connected on Earth. Each of us, therefore, has the reciprocal responsibility to extend a helping hand to as many people as possible. We do not necessarily need to have a blood relationship or a business or other formal relationship with those we help in life. The only imperative of true helpfulness is that it has to be genuine and spring from the heart. We should always be prepared to help others in any way we can, because not only does giving help uplift us, but receiving it enables people to see life in a positive and loving way.

There are diverse forms of help that we can offer to others. A lot of us might think in terms of monetary help and, yes, in certain cases this is the kind of assistance that is required. In other kinds of situations, however, help might mean showing the right path to someone, listening to his or her problems and grievances, and providing encouragement to boost low spirits. We can also help our friends and neighbours when they are sick or dealing with a family member who needs constant care and attention. We might offer our help to buy groceries, to pick up medications, or to watch a sick person while the caregiver gets a few hours' break. Just lending our physical presence in times of need to friends, colleagues, or family is more than enough to show support during a crisis. Sometimes a genuine offer to help someone, a promise to be there for another person, is all that is needed for reassurance. Help may also be the kind of support and collaboration that makes for effective teamwork in the office or other workplace. Help can be in any form, as long as it contributes to the success of others as they take their spiritual journeys on Earth.

There is no limit to the quantity and kind of help that we can, and should, extend to others. By the same token, help is also available to each of us in abundance. When we seek help, God will send it in the right manner and through the right person. We must each consider ourselves to be worthy in the universe and remember, too, that every other soul we meet is similarly worthy. We are born from one Creator and our role as human beings seeking spiritual growth is to support one another as we face the challenges of earthly existence.

Though we do not know it in our physical minds, our souls each may have dependencies on, and specific connections with, other souls. We may have made soul promises before we were born to serve certain other souls. Of course, these contracts are not handed over to us at the time of our birth, but they are imbedded in our higher minds. Only when we tap into our higher minds will we discover our connections with other souls.

Extending help when needed is one of the most basic measures of friendship. A true friendship is determined by how well our friends stand by and support us in our toughest and most distressful times and, conversely, how well we support them in their difficult situations. There are the kind of friends who stand by us regardless of the kind of problems we might have—anything from health to financial or legal issues. And then there are the other kind who will become distant and fearful of how others might perceive them if they maintain ties with people in crisis. While the latter kind of scenario can be disappointing, there is no need to give in to dejection. We must draw upon our higher minds and strive for the consciousness to understand that our friends have reasons for turning away for us. We can still continue to love them at a soul level.

Experiences of being rejected or isolated can be valuable lessons for each of us. We can resolve to avoid similarly drawing away from friends who need us and to be considerate and compassionate with people who are facing difficult life challenges. Thus a disappointing situation can both teach us the value of friendship and awaken our spiritual qualities of consideration and compassion. This is yet another example of how every unpleasant earthly experience is a lesson to be learned. No experience is wasted on Earth.

The Importance of Pure Intentions
Lending a helping hand to friends does not have to entail enormous sacrifice. Nor does it have to be difficult or tedious. It only has to be purely intended, free from any self-interested ulterior motive.

From my own experience, I recall when some young friends had a new baby. Another friend came up with an idea that it would be a nice gesture if one family cooked food for each day and delivered it to the busy new parents. The plan was to take turns doing this each day for a month. One person took charge of coordinating the food preferences, organizing who would cook on each day, and sending out reminders. Everything went perfectly, as planned. The couple receiving the meals were appreciative, and we continued doing the same thing for other friends when they had new babies. Granted, most of the work was done by the wives, and the husbands just bought groceries and delivered food. But what mattered was that everyone pitched in with goodwill and the true desire to ease the lives of friends.

When we help others in this way—that is, with pure intentions and no expectation of getting something in return—it contributes to the progress of our souls. When, however, we assist someone with an intent to

LIVING WITH CONSCIOUSNESS

gain something for our own selfish needs—for example, money, glory, or power—it is not truly help. The spiritual laws are very specific on this point.

Similarly, supporting one person while messing up the life of another does not qualify as help in any spiritual sense. Unfortunately, this sort of "help" abounds in the world of corporate politics. Here is just one, not-too-unusual example:

Don is the VP of Logistics for a freight forwarding company. Tim is the Manager of Operations, reporting directly to Don. The company is expanding its operations to include a new position of District Manager of Operations. Harvey is currently assigned by Don to work with Tim and to assist him as operations expand.

Tim has a master's degree in business administration. Harvey has an undergraduate degree in business. Harvey, aware that a new position of District Manager is being created, manipulates Don by saying negative things about Tim and the way operations are being handled. Don does not like Tim, since he is knowledgeable about operations and cannot be manipulated into faking operational reports to the board in order to cast Don in an unrealistically favourable light. On the other hand, Don has found Harvey to be amenable to ethically questionable practices to help Don enhance his power and reputation with the board. The question is, how can Don bring Harvey on board as District Manager when he has fewer qualifications than Tim, and has not worked with the company for more than six months?

Don connects with Alison, the Director of Human Resources, and tells her of his plan to bring Harvey on board as the new District Manager of Operations. Alison has always admired Don and the way he presents himself. She likes his ruthless manner of achieving whatever he wants and getting things accomplished. She figures that if she can find a way to help Don, her effort will assist her own career advancement. A few days later Alison informs Don that she has created a new job description and has selected a panel of five people, including herself, to interview for the position. She also tells Don that the panel has made aware of his preference for Harvey and advised to favour him over Tim.

As expected, Tim and Harvey both apply for the District Manager position. All of the people on the interviewing panel vote in favour of Harvey, except for one person who had a change of heart, as his conscience would not permit him to favour the wrong candidate. Harvey is selected and everyone, except Tim, is happy. Now it is Alison's turn to seek Don's help in return for her assistance with hiring Harvey. Don complies, forms another interviewing panel, and maneuvers its members into selecting Alison as VP of Human Resources.

The "help" given in this example is of course three people mutually promoting each other's external power. Don, Harvey, and Alison each made intentional choices that were not right and entirely in their own self-interest. Not only is this not true helpfulness but it is a glaring instance of building negative karma. When we help someone achieve a negative goal, and that person provides negative help in return, the cycle of negativity continues and more and more people are dragged into the net. And the cycle does not stay confined to the workspace. People like Don, Harvey, and Alison take their distorted energies home with them and contaminate their own private lives. In their exaggerated sense of power, they become increasingly disconnected from their loved ones until, in the end, they literally become lost souls.

With current unfavourable economic trends and high unemployment rates, we are all likely to encounter people, perhaps especially youths, who are seeking jobs. If we find ourselves in positions that gives us hiring power, we should refrain from giving jobs in circumstances where we might benefit politically or otherwise by our decisions. We are in such positions for a reason and should use our power for good and make our hiring decisions in the true spirit of helpfulness, and with due consideration of the merits of the job seekers. When someone comes to us for help with getting a job, we need to consider ourselves to be worthy and lucky that we have been chosen by God to be instruments to contribute in this way to others' lives. These are God-given opportunities for our own souls and for us as earthly beings to do the right thing—because real help of any kind has to be offered on a soul level. There is no other way.

Life Is a Gift

Things happen at the right time. There is a perfect moment for each and every thing, including those "aha" moments in life that set us onto new and productive pathways. Life is a gift to each of us so that we can grow spiritually by selflessly serving others. This should not in fact be difficult for any of us. For despite some people's tendency to work only for their own ends, the truth is that it is in our nature as human beings to help others.

The other good news is that being helpful and improving spiritually are cyclical in a positive way. That is, the more we help others, the more we grow spiritually, and with such growth, the more giving we become and the more strongly inclined to keep on helping others—and so on... Accordingly, as we increasingly call upon and develop our higher minds, we grow in our capacity for compassion, empathy, patience, friendship, and love. All of this, of course, not only results from our earthly actions but also happens at soul level. For ultimately, it is our souls that push us to acquire virtue and to act on it in everyday life. In other words, even one small good deed in earthly life is always a profound act with lasting spiritual benefits.

When we consistently make choices that develop us spiritually, we gain inner peace, which is a powerful factor in coping with any challenge that life might present. When we are truly at peace, we take earthly problems in our stride. Emotionally and spiritually, we go with the flow of life, taking right action and making good choices. As long as we continue to do so—each of us in our own individually unique way—we will keep on growing in spiritual awareness. In this way we come to know our own true selves as we progressively fulfill the very purpose for which we received the gift of life.

Gratitude

Gratitude. It is a simple but powerful word that carries deep spiritual meaning. Gratitude means being content with, and thankful for, all the possessions, advantages, people, and blessings that we each have in life.

A grateful person never looks at what is missing from his or her life, because this in itself would be an ungrateful approach. When we start enumerating what we don't have, we are making an implied comparison between life as it is and life as our physical minds might desire it to be. Inevitably, along with such a comparison comes greed to have more. This creates dissatisfaction and makes us prone to dismissing and not enjoying what we do have in life.

Sometimes we are also filled with jealousy or envy when we fall into the trap of comparing our own lives to the supposedly better lives that others enjoy. When we succumb to this frame of mind, we are likely to make mean-spirited, unconscious choices as we go about our daily lives. For example, if we envy someone else's job, we might spread negative rumors about that person or even speak ill of him or her to the team leader or manager. How far such behaviour takes us from gratitude. And to what end? All that can result is unpleasantness for another human being, at the expense of our own spiritual well-being.

The best way to face life's challenges is the grateful way. When we cherish the work that we do, we perform with diligence. When we value every moment that life gives us, we use our time wisely. When we are content with our relationships, we nurture them. When we approach every aspect of life with grateful hearts, not only do we cope well but we also reap the benefits in emotional health and spiritual growth.

Unfortunately, rather than cultivating gratitude, human beings have a tendency to complain, and the more we get out of life, the more we want. Some people seem to be born complainers and are never satisfied. Their energy frequency is always negative and they are never able to fully comprehend the meaning of life. Their typical response to all constructive suggestions is, "Yeah, but . . ." They are not open to new possibilities and do not truly want to move forward, because that would give them less reason to indulge in their preferred pastime—complaining. The lesson that we can all learn from the complainers is simple: Don't do it. Complaining is a waste of energy, a betrayal of the higher self, and a sure way to weaken connection with God.

Gratitude emerges in various ways. It can touch us when we encounter another person's pain and sorrows in life. When I listen to stories on television and video, especially on the "The Purple Couch" or *Oprah's Lifeclass or Super Soul Sunday*, I gain a deep realization that my pain and suffering are nothing compared to the traumas that many others have gone through. At such times, I feel blessed and grateful for the life I am leading with my family.

We also need to look at every personal experience of our own as an opportunity to feel gratitude. This is easy when things are going well, and difficult when we are caught up in life's more challenging situations. I use the times when life is a struggle as opportunities to silently observe nature, admiring the beauty of God's creations and feeling peace of mind returning to me. In difficult times, I also put in extra effort to maintain good relationships with my family and friends. I relax my physical mind by reading books, either to upgrade my career skills and talents or to improve my grasp of spiritual knowledge. Most helpful for me is to sit in silence, to meditate, and to let my higher mind help me flow with my life. Once I have achieved this meditative state, nothing in life can upset me or my soul, and I feel grateful for the gift of life and all that comes with it.

Grateful people carry with them a high level of positive energy. They are calm, serene, and able to think through problems strategically, to find better solutions for their lives. They are also healthy, vigorous, and eager to enjoy every moment with joy and tranquility. Grateful people cope with life's challenges purposefully, because they are always connected to their own souls.

Gratitude, then, is a quality of mind and heart that is directly connected to contentment at the soul level. If we let it, it comes naturally to us and can readily become a positive habit in our everyday existence. As we face life's challenges, we can each reaffirm our gratitude by incorporating the following prayer into our daily thoughts and meditations:

Prayer of Gratitude

I look at my life and see how grateful I am today, for without you, my Lord, I would have moved further away from you.

You held me in your arms when things got tough and held me tight till I was able to take charge of my life.

Day in and day out, you protected me from all harm, and I swear that I would have been harmed without you in my life.

You gave me the courage to hold my head high and allowed me to weather the darkest of times.

You gave me love when I needed it the most in my life, for without that love there was no hope for my life.

I am thankful for the journey you have mapped out for me, and I promise you that I will serve you till the last day of my life.

I am thankful for the love I have from my family and friends, because it is love that keeps me going and makes me stronger every day.

I love you with all my heart and pray that you will show me the right path day by day.

Lord, bless me, protect me, and keep me safe; for without your blessings and protection I would have gone astray.

For all this and more, Lord, I am truly and always grateful.

• • •

Inspirational Connections

- **To cope with life's challenges, surrender to God and go with the flow of life.**
- **Have faith.**
- **Be patient.**
- **Act with love.**
- **Help others; do so without ulterior, self-serving motives.**
- **Know that life is a gift; use it wisely.**
- **Be grateful.**

12
One Universal God

While I know myself as a creation of God, I am also obligated to realize and remember that everyone else and everything else are also God's creation.

—Maya Angelou

THERE IS ONLY ONE GOD but many ways of reaching God. In his greatness, he is everywhere, in each and every thing. His presence fills each moment. He lives in our hearts and spirits. He is loving and forgiving in life. If we stay connected with God and our own souls, we will always follow his path and his direction. When we are connected in this way, we make the best possible choices for our lives and our souls. All of our actions and decisions are conscious, for God's essence within us is all-powerful.

Appreciating the Greatness of God
God is in every smile of those that are faithful. With God by our sides, we can smile even when we have sorrow and pain. We can smile when we are missing something in life, or when we have lost our earthly possessions and power, for we have God in his greatness always with us. We can smile for the troubled past, because the present is bright and the future gets brighter with each passing day. We can smile for what we have, and for the perfect lives that we enjoy, which are precious not only to us but also to our loved ones. No matter what life brings, we can smile in the presence of troubles as well as joys, because we are connected to God and his essence.

In his greatness, God helps us learn to live with dignity, with peace, and most of all, with humility. When we face tough times, we need to turn to God, for he will lead the way, show us the right path, and give us the strength to go through our ordeals on Earth. God is always training us with ever-increasing rigour, so that we can serve him in his work and purpose. He wants us to be perfect, loving, faithful, trustworthy, honest, and peaceful. He wants us to follow the path of righteousness and lead others in the same direction. Most of all, he wants us to become worthy of doing his work in life, in order that we can spread knowledge of him and help share his wisdom.

God resides in all of us. He knows our good and bad points. He knows our strengths and weaknesses. If we follow him and his light, he will show us the way to move closer to him. He is powerful and he is the mightiest of mightiest. He is divine and he is the supreme creator of the universe. Nothing is possible without God and his light. We are here on Earth to grow spiritually and we might as well make the best use of our time to improve, to evolve, and to progress along the spiritual path.

Rumi, the thirteenth-century Persian poet and mystic (1207–1273), believed that human beings are capable of rising to great spiritual heights. Even if we are at the lowest levels of spirituality, when we turn to God's greatness, we begin the ascent to grace:

> Knock, And He'll open the door.
> Vanish, And He'll make you shine like the sun.
> Fall, And He'll raise you to the heavens.
> Become nothing, And He'll turn you into everything.

As souls, we have chosen to be born so that, with God's help, we can overcome our weak spiritual qualities, cultivate the goodness in us, and eradicate the dark and evil forces of negativity to which we may be drawn. God wants us to fight the negativity so that we improve and move closer to him. If we are determined, he will guide us to success. He will never force us to go in his direction, however, for we have the free will to choose what we want in life. The more that we make poor decisions and act wrongly, the longer it will take us to move forward on the spiritual path, and the longer it will take to merge with the Creator. Our choices in life therefore matter, for through them we shape our destinies and either move toward or away from God. Because all of humanity is his creation, God wants us to thrive and to move forward and upward along the one path that leads to him. As the Swiss theologian Hans Urs von Balthasar (1905–1988) expressed it, "What you are is God's gift to you, what you become is your gift to God."

For each of us to become a worthy gift for God, we must begin with faith. From faith emanate all the other qualities that help us progress toward God: acceptance of life's problems, humility, kindness, and compassion for others. As fallible beings, we will often stumble, fall, and backslide on the path to God, but by always living with faith in God's greatness we will eventually reach our destination.

Our Connection to God

How we each conduct ourselves on Earth shows the strength of our individual connection to God. The more giving, gentle, selfless, caring, compassionate, and empathetic we are, the more connected we stay to God. For God has all these qualities, and when we incorporate them into our own day-to-day lives, we are strengthening our connection to God. We focus more on his love and kindness, and thus become more selfless, caring, and compassionate in life. God resides in all of us, but as unique individuals, it is up to each one of us to find our own way to seek, discover, and connect with him.

Sometimes our connection is weakened or broken because things are not going well in our lives. There are the times when we need to make the greatest effort to remain faithful and to rebuild our connection with God. It helps when we remember that everything happens for the uplifting of our souls, which are always longing for purity. Our souls want to forgive others and to move ahead; and the way to do so is to open our minds and grasp that God is in each and everything we see, touch, smell, and feel. God is knowable—he is not hidden in caves or beyond reach on some mountain peak. He is sitting right inside our hearts. When we follow our higher minds, we will always be connected to his essence, his light, and his love.

Since God is the divine creator of the entire universe, he loves each of us. If we love him in return, we will never feel unloved—indeed, we will be engulfed in love from all sides. When we love God, we attract the love of other people. And when we can see the love in God, then it is easier for us to see love in all human beings on Earth. When we love all, we are loved in return. When we love God, we feel his love in each and every action we undertake, in each and every thought we generate, and in each and every word we convey to others. Love of God is thus at the core of every positive human interaction in which we might engage.

Because we are all connected to God, we are also all connected to his power. He is always there for us when we need him the most. We need not, and should not, ever doubt this. To give in to doubt is to encourage negativity and that moves us further from God's power and protection. But to hold to faith is to benefit always from God's power and protection. This remains true whether we are suffering from problems and tragedies in life or enjoying success and peace.

There are people who believe in God but only seek his help in times of troubles. Others are more apt to believe in God when they achieve something great in life. And then there are those who are faithful to God at all times and grateful for everything in life. They are grateful for the gifts they have and the things they can share. They are grateful for the love, peace, and happiness that encompasses them in their life. These people also ask God for strength and mercy when the going gets tough. These people connect with him to support them as they go through their ordeals, pain, and suffering on Earth. These people, the truly and unwaveringly faithful, have God in their hearts, minds, and spirits twenty-four seven. They know that the Lord is their saviour. They know that they can overcome all obstacles if God is by their side.

If we want to be closer to God, we need to stay connected to him. We strengthen the connection every time that we serve others. Every helpful action that we perform is an opportunity to bond with another soul and connect with God. While many choose the godly path of connection, others choose to ignore God and his spirit. If we choose to dismiss God from our hearts and daily lives, then we are cultivating the ignorance of our own spirits. We are curbing the advancement of our souls and degrading our own spirits.

Wisdom lives in our souls. Our job as earthly beings is to tap into it. All we need to do is to open our higher minds and let the spiritual knowledge speak to us. When we listen in this way we are blessed. When we act on the guidance we thus receive, we forge an increasingly stronger connection to God and grow ever closer to him for the duration of our journeys on Earth.

We Are All Connected

God looks after everyone's interest. No one is stranded, not even the person asking for a dollar or two to survive another day. Someone or other always steps forward to help another soul in need. This is because we are all connected at soul level and we feel the pain in our own souls when we see someone's suffering in life. It makes no difference whether they are family, friends, or total strangers. Even though we don't know someone in this lifetime, we can nonetheless feel his or her cry for help, mercy, and love.

When driven by compassion, a person can look at others through the eyes of the soul and connect with them on a soul-to-soul basis. At such times, there is a flow of energy that emanates from one soul to another for the benefit of both. This happened to a friend of mine on what began as an ordinary day:

My friend and I had gone grocery shopping at Costco. During the drive back to our homes, we stopped at a traffic signal, and my friend noticed a boy in his early twenties who was in the other lane, seeking monetary help from passersby. Normally, my friend prefers to provide help by donating money to food banks, the children's hospital, or other charities; he is not in favour of helping someone on the road. I am not sure exactly what resonated at his soul level that day, but he immediately told me to call the boy over. He then opened his wallet and gave him enough money to buy a good meal.

When the traffic lights turned green and I was driving away, I could not help but comment on what had just occurred. "This is very unlike you," I said. "I have never seen your compassionate side before, and I am very impressed." I must have repeated this statement three times or more. Finally he told me: "I don't know what came over me when

I saw that boy. I felt something deep in my soul and spirit, and my soul just wanted to reach out to him."

I suggested that the boy could be a past-life connection. "You know him as a soul, and your soul can see his soul and feel his pain and presence. Or he might have helped you somewhere in your previous life." Whatever is the precise explanation for this incident, there is no doubt that it moved my friend's soul to such an extent that he has since become more compassionate in life.

Trusting God and His Plan for the Universe
We must never doubt the existence of God. The moment we have such doubt we must banish it from our minds and strive to increase our faith in God Almighty. We need to trust that there is a reason and a higher purpose in everything he does. His judgement is pure and selfless. He works in the best interest of each soul and supports us as we develop the qualities that we need in order to progress spiritually. God wants us all closer to his energy and presence. He wants us all to improve spiritually so that we can serve him in the best possible way. He wants us to rise spiritually so that we become pillars of society and towers of strength for our families. He wants us all to lead with compassion, kindness, humility, fairness, and justice. He has only pure intentions, which are for the benefit and progress of our souls.

Accordingly, each human soul has only one true agenda: spiritual improvement. If this means enduring obstacles and suffering in life, we should not be deterred. On the contrary, the greater the suffering, the faster the soul purifies and progresses. Whatever happens in our lives, the role of each of us is to trust in God, accept all the hurdles that block our paths, and do our best to stride over them. When we thus lead our lives with purpose we can be happy, calm, and at peace, for we are in harmony with God's plan.

Everything works in accordance with God's plan, his purpose, and his direction. We cannot interfere with his plan, for if we were to do so, we would create an imbalance in the universe. And just one small imbalance can upset our lives and, in the process, impact the lives of others. This is why it is imperative that we learn to trust God. It is not a difficult lesson, for all we really need to understand is that God has a plan, that we are an integral part of it, and that God has devised it out of pure intent, in our own best interest. In the end, to believe in God is to assimilate this lesson. Nothing more, nothing less—it's what faith is all about.

Forces of Darkness and Light

Throughout time, the world has been faced with two fundamental choices: to accept the force of light, which shines with the presence of God, his essence, love, kindness, compassion, mercy, and forgiveness; or to succumb to the force of darkness, which draws us into a vortex of negativity that makes us mean, greedy, vengeful, vindictive, uncompassionate, unmerciful, and unforgiving. These are the two forces that are in constant struggle over the souls of human beings on Earth.

Our consciousness permits either choice—darkness or light. With a high enough level of spiritual understanding, we can fight darkness and emerge into the light. But if our understanding is wrong, and we are not aware of our own consciousness, we are apt to choose the path of darkness, for it can gratify our materialistic desires. The path of light might seem to be difficult, but its rewards are the greater gifts of peace and happiness. For the light is the spirit of God.

The question is, how do we find and follow the light? Being humble helps us recognize the light. Opening our higher minds shows us the light. Speaking or acting from the depths of the soul awakens our spirits. And then we follow the light that resides within us.

When we follow the darkness and give licence to the dark side of ourselves, we are alienating our souls from God. We are withdrawing our souls from his presence and moving into a place that is empty and shallow. The force of darkness is very pleasing to our egos, because it is only through the dark side of our nature that we feed the ego. The ego is never pleased when we speak or act from the depths of the soul. This is because the ego then loses its powerful image and importance. It becomes dull, charmless, and diminished in value. Little is left of it, for it has nothing to fight over, compare itself to, or complain about.

When the ego has nothing to occupy it, we start moving into a space that allows us to listen to the wise, calm voice of our higher minds. This is now a fresh beginning, a new turn to advance our own particular journeys on Earth, for we are moving with the spirit in each of us. The darkness loses its importance and the light of God illuminates the pathway to spiritual growth.

• • •

Inspirational Connections

- There is only one God.
- God's greatness shows everywhere and in everything.
- You are connected to God and to his power.
- Through God, you are connected to all other souls; have compassion for everyone.
- Trust in God, for he has plan for the universe, and you are an integral part of the plan.
- Forces of darkness and light surround you at all times.
- Abandon your ego and choose God's light—it illuminates the spiritual path.

13
The Soul

Goodbyes are only for those who love with their eyes. Because for those who love with their heart and soul there is no such thing as separation.

—*Rumi*

THE SOUL IS A CREATION of God and imbued with all the purity, goodness and essence of God. The soul is the real you—that is, your true self. The soul is the spiritual body in each of us, and it lives for eternity. The soul has various ways to improve spiritually. Taking a birth on Earth is one of those ways, and thus we are all here for the same purpose: spiritual growth.

Birth and Death

The soul begins its journey on Earth by taking a birth and ends its journey when it breathes its last breath on Earth. The ending of the last breath is termed *death* in our earthly world and the soul moves back into the spirit world, its original place of birth. The soul decides the number of years it will live on Earth. The soul makes a plan as to when to take birth, which family to take birth with, and what he or she wants to accomplish in order to advance spiritually—that is, what training, tests, and life experiences will be required to repay past karma. The soul also decides the precise way that the individual will evolve and whom he or she wants to help on Earth.

The soul's earthly journey thus has deep meaning, but as fallible human beings we often forget this. Our souls are meant to progress during our earthly journeys, but often we get caught up in pain and suffering or bogged down with worldly and materialistic distractions, and we forget life's true purpose. The soul is born for a specific purpose and must devote a certain amount of time to fulfilling that purpose on Earth. The time is fixed before taking birth and if the soul's mission is not completed, it will be a life not well lived and the waste of an earthly journey. There are extreme cases when a soul will exchange his particular life for someone else's life. This is done at a soul level. The person whose life has no meaning and wants to move to the spirit world trades his life with another soul who has a meaningful mission and needs more time to fulfill that mission on Earth.

Death is the creation of a new life for the soul; it is a continuation of each of our spirits. The only difference is that once we die, we continue our journeys and the progression of our souls in the spirit world. The soul is never born without a purpose. If a soul takes a birth for only a few years, or even a few minutes or seconds, it is because he or she has chosen to take birth only for that selected period of time. The timing of life and death always resides with each soul, and depends upon the progress he or she wants to make, the lessons chosen, and the impact that each soul wants to make on other souls by being born and living on Earth. These are the choices of the soul's free will, and each soul is the master of his or her life journey on Earth.

There is thus no need to blame God when our loved ones move early to the spirit world. There is no need to feel guilt that a soul has left us because our actions were not worthy or we were not loving parents. No matter how briefly a soul might stay on Earth, the time is precious, because each soul has the capability of touching the lives of other souls, to bring about changes in their behaviours and attitudes. Most of all, for whatever earthly time they have, all souls must strive to inspire love as widely as possible, for it is love that connects one soul to another, and the bond of love lasts forever.

Ups and downs, troubles and turmoil, grief and misery, but also happiness, pleasure, peace, and contentment—these are all part of life. We cannot have the good things and not the bad. As souls, we cannot select only goodness for our lives. If our lives always went smoothly, there would be no evolution for our souls. With no ups and downs, life would be stagnant and have no meaning, because experiencing our earthly journeys to their full potential is the only way to live meaningfully.

We must always try to remember that our souls have each chosen to be born on Earth so that we can grow spiritually. To achieve this greatest purpose of our lives, we need to fulfill other related purposes. These include learning from our life experiences, improving on negative qualities, and repaying our karma. Being close to loved ones is yet another of the soul's purposes, as is helping others to discover and to stay on the spiritual path.

Once the soul's spiritual purpose is fulfilled in any given lifetime, the soul will leave the earthly plane and move into the spiritual plane. Death is merely the shedding of our physical bodies on Earth and a means for the soul to transition into the spirit world. Unlike the body, which is mortal, the soul is immortal. It never dies, for it is a part of God; and as God is infinite, so too is the life of each soul.

Rebirth
We need to be ready for a rebirth. If we want to take a rebirth, we have to put in our request to the highest good soul of the particular spirit realm to which each of us belongs. In each case, he or she will assist three wise souls to help us map out our own journey on Earth. The three wise souls will be the ultimate authorities for the earthly journey that we each take.

Prior to rebirth, there are discussions about what the soul wants to achieve and learn; the amount of karma to be repaid must also be determined. A plan is developed, but not in a single sitting. Depending on the particular soul, and the kind of journey he or she wants to undertake, it can take several meetings over significant duration if the soul is adamant about what he or she desires to accomplish. The plan includes a lot of detail—the soul's likes and dislikes; who the parents and family will be; how much earthly bonding and love will be sought; and the extent to which the soul will be teaching and helping other souls. Repaying of karma is only one reason for rebirth; the greater reason is to learn to live in peace and compassion and to help other souls on Earth.

After it is final, the plan for the earthly journey is documented and stored. Later, when the soul comes back to the spirit world, he or she can compare the plan to what has been set down in the *akashic* record—the aggregation of all human experience, according to theosophy and some traditions of Buddhism. This process of comparison helps souls see their flaws and what they achieved, or not, on Earth. At this stage, souls assess their shortcomings and decide whether they want to overcome them by taking a rebirth or by advancing in the spirit world.

Depending on our consciousness and soul progress, we might overachieve on Earth and exceed what we had taken birth for; on the other hand, because of free will, negative thinking, and pride, we might also deviate from the course of our journey and regress spiritually. Although the spiritual laws apply to all, the particular ways that a soul might achieve or deviate from his or her earthly purpose vary from soul to soul. If a soul is going in the wrong direction, his loved ones on Earth and in the spirit world will try to help him get back on track in his journey. There is always some help and support available, but eventually what happens to each and every soul is the result of their own individual choice, connection with God, faith, and love for God. Each journey is special. Each journey touches the lives of other souls and has an impact in the universe in some form or another.

The spirit world keeps a track of the number of people who will be allowed to take a rebirth. The high good souls of the spirit world are in charge of monitoring this balance in the universe, which takes in both Earth and the spirit world. The number of souls in the spirit world will be higher than people born on Earth, for there are other souls involved in various projects in the spirit world. The masters or rulers of each realm constantly monitor the need for and requirements of birth and rebirth. All the necessary information and knowledge is stored for reference and cross-reference.

Death
At the end of the earthly journey, the soul breaks its connection from the inactive physical body and moves into the spirit world. Calling this, as we do, *death*, is not strictly accurate. For, while the physical body dies, the soul lives forever. Once the body ceases to house the soul, the soul returns to the spirit world with wisdom and knowledge if it has progressed spiritually. If the soul has failed in its purpose due to bad actions on Earth, it still returns to the spirit world, but in a state of regressed spirituality.

Death is not a permanent solution for the spirit. It is only a transition from Earth to the spirit world. Death means evolution and rejuvenation for the spirit. This is a process that no one can escape. Earthly death is a requirement for the evolution of the soul. This reminds me of a story that I learnt in school:

A young woman married to a wealthy businessman. Her only child, a one-year-old boy, fell sick and died. She was overcome with grief and could not believe that the son she loved so much was truly dead. She sought out someone who had the power to bring her son back to life. She came across a Buddhist monk who suggested that she go and see Gautama Buddha. She told her story to Buddha, who listened with compassion and patience. Buddha said that he could help her if she could get four or five mustard seeds from any family in town whose house had not had a death in it. She roamed around the town, knocking on each door. Everyone was willing to give her the mustard seeds but, in each house, someone or the other had passed away. While searching in vain for a house where there had been no death, she came to realize that death is a part of life, and it is inevitable and it is inescapable.

When we face the death of a loved one, we can take comfort from knowing that while our physical connection ends, our spiritual connection and love for that person stays forever because the soul lives in eternity. I learned this at a young age when I had the experience of losing friends, family members, and relatives. The most gripping loss I faced was when my grandfather passed away. I was very close to him, closer than my other siblings. I felt the loss of his physical presence and energy, and I missed his inspiring and supportive words. But I also had the comforting awareness that he was alive in spirit because, in India, from an early age we are taught the principles of birth, rebirth, karma, death, and spirit. Over the years, I have seen many more people die during my journey on Earth: my good friend, who died in a motorbike accident; my mom's friend's husband, who died trying to save someone when they were swimming in the sea; my dad and mom sisters; my dad; my spiritual teacher, Khorshed

Bhavnagri and her husband Rumi Bhavnagri; and many more souls who were close to me. I miss them but know that they had to leave Earth, since they had completed their journeys.

Death means birth in the spirit world. Our earthly journeys end with death but we continue our spiritual journeys by doing work in the spirit world. We might agree to be spirit guides, mentors, or guardian angels. We might help others transition to the spirit world once they are dead. We might also attend to other activities, such as expanding our knowledge of spirituality—there is no end to learning.

As human beings, we should be focussed on leading spiritual lives, so that when our time comes to move to the spirit world, we have no regrets about our earthly journeys. We should not take with us the knowledge that we did not enjoy our life and were not loving, compassionate, selfless, and forgiving. The biggest regret we might have is that we did not make peace with our friends and families, and did not restore broken ties with people whom we love from the heart but became estranged from due to our individual differences.

Creation of Soul and Purpose

God creates souls for interaction with one another, and to serve him and assist with his plans for all the universe. The soul is a part of God just as a child is a part of the mother and father. Each soul is created with the same level of consciousness. Each soul has the same spiritual knowledge of all the laws of God Almighty; each soul is created for perfection. God is fair to all and gives equal opportunity for all souls to grow spiritually.

After our creation, we are endowed with free will; the ability to make individual choices in all circumstances. We build negative karma by choosing to take the wrong spiritual path. Conversely, following the right spiritual path brings us closer to God. The choices are always entirely our own—whether they are conscious and wise or unconscious and negative. Many of us have heard that good attracts good, and bad attracts bad. Similarly, positive choices strengthen our spirits and negative choices weaken our spirits, which draws us up and down, creating high or low energy in and around us in whatever we do in life. The soul is the guiding force that leads us to our higher minds. If we awaken the higher mind, we awaken the spirit within us. If we ignore the higher mind, we weaken the spirit that resides in us. Knowing that we are a part of God and his energy, we need to strive to make sure that all our actions are conscious—that our thoughts are positive; that our words inspire, encourage, and uplift the spirits of others; and that all our deeds spring from the heart, with a selfless desire to help others in life.

The whole purpose of each of our journeys is to serve others from the day we are born. The sight of a newborn child, for example, brings a smile to the faces of the onlookers. As we move forward in life, we please others with our childish and playful actions. These actions may bring joy to another child, friend, sibling, parents, grandparents, colleagues, or twin soul. Even though we are young, we are serving someone in some respect. The service is done at a soul level; the resultant happiness is also created at a soul level and transmitted to other souls. Our duty never ends; our service never finishes. As we move ahead in life, we might help someone with their studies or provide a listening ear to a friend in need. We grow, become educated, find employment, and progress in life. We serve the place we work, the people who work for us, under us, and above us. The chain continues. It is a never-ending process, and if we really are spiritually aware, there is never a missed opportunity to serve someone or other in life. We serve someone with a smile, greeting, helping hand, and encouraging words of appreciation. We can serve others through our actions in each and every aspect of daily life.

When we serve others, we connect with them at a soul level. The love that others show us in this life stays with our souls forever. The effect is cumulative, for the love and sacrifice by others in our previous lives also stays within our souls. As we are being born and reborn to learn our spiritual lessons, we not only extend our connection to other souls but also to God. The more we learn to serve others during earthly lifetimes, the stronger and closer grows our connection to God.

Developing Positive Soul Qualities

Peace. One of the highest qualities to develop as a soul is the ability to generate peace. We can only do so if we have cultivated such other attributes as love, kindness, compassion, and patience. The state of being at peace arises from the combination of all other positive attributes. We cannot generate peace for ourselves or others if our minds are filled with ego. If we are trying to justify our actions and behaviours, or if we are on the lookout to prove ourselves right on each and every point, then we are being ego driven. Peace means letting go of ego and other qualities of mind that hold no value for our souls and spirits. Peace means being bold enough to standing up for the truth while remaining conciliatory enough to avoid spirit-depleting conflict. Peace means having the courage and humility to accept our flaws and to take full responsibility for our actions in life.

Peace and love are from the same family. If we love someone, we will always aim for peace, because our love is more powerful than the urge to be always right. Through love, we develop the restraint to avoid actions or words that could put our relationships at risk. When we operate in love and peace, we are happy with all outcomes that life might offer. This is the way to lasting inner peace.

Lao Tzu, the great poet and philosopher of ancient China, has said that if we want to create peace in the world, there must be peace in our hearts:

> If there is to be peace in the world, there must be peace in nations.
>
> If there is to be peace in the nations, there must be peace in cities.
>
> If there is to be peace in the cities, there must be peace between neighbours.
>
> If there is to be peace between neighbours, there must be peace in the home.
>
> If there is to be peace in the home, there must be peace in the heart.

Tolerance. We all have a lot to learn in life. We are all connected in order to learn and to grow spiritually; and we all need to tolerate one another in life so that we can reduce our negative soul characteristics. Just as we need to accept what life offers us, we also need to be tolerant of the foibles of others. For, like us, other people are on Earth according to a plan for their improvement. When we strive to see other people's good qualities and to love them for what they are, and not for what we want them to be, then we all move forward on our journeys.

Love. Love and tolerance are closely related. The connection between two souls is love; the connection within any positive relationships is love in some form. Love helps us to accept the positive and the negative in another person. Love is the universal truth and the most powerful and widely traded currency in the universe. Love helps us gain empathy with others and empty our hearts of hatred, envy, and vengefulness. To love is to tolerate.

Forgiveness. In an ideal world, forgiveness would be simple and natural for all of us. In reality, however, many people lead their lives with grudges, fears, hatred, and resentments. These negative feelings are good neither for our souls nor our physical bodies. Like a worm in an apple, hatred and other unforgiving feelings stop the soul's progress and deplete the body's energy, sometimes to the point of serious illness. There is only one way to remove the gnawing worm, and that way is the path of forgiveness. By forgiving others, we purify our souls, lighten our spirits, soften our hearts, heal our physical minds, and restore vigour to our bodies. Forgiveness brings peace and serenity to us at all levels—soul, spirit, heart, mind, and body—making our natures more pleasing to ourselves, to others, and to God.

How does forgiveness work? The moment that we forgive someone, we release a positive energy that is so powerful that it reaches the soul of the person who is forgiven. He or she will feel the difference in mind, body, and spirit, will feel a lessening of pain and lightening of heart. Forgiveness is not a simple act of accepting an apology. Forgiveness is only achieved when one soul overcomes hatred, anger, desire for revenge, jealousy, and all other negative feelings. At this point, the person takes charge of his or her own thoughts, emotions, and behaviour. He or she feels a strength of soul that pours out to forgive the other soul. Negative energy is replaced with kindness, understanding, compassion, and wisdom, from which feelings of forgiveness flows and embraces the other soul with love and purity.

Forgiveness is an act that has to resonate at a soul level. When we forgive, we heal our souls and, in turn, help other souls heal. Forgiveness shines a positive light into the universe and our own souls. With forgiveness comes peace, and the soul sends a powerful message: *All is well. I forgive you and love you for what you are.* There are no boundaries to forgiveness. Distance only separates us from the physical presence of another person. When we forgive from the soul, the other person feels it at soul level, no matter how great the distance between us might be.

Forgive all, for forgiveness is the ultimate act of love in every relationship. When we forgive others we also forgive our own selves and repair our hurts. Forgiveness heals everyone concerned, and helps raise the consciousness of ourselves and others. Nowhere is the need for forgiveness stronger than in situations of divorce where children are involved:

When John was nine, his parents, Karl and Stacy, separated and divorced. John took the separation very hard and, full of rage, refused to see his father; he often spoke harshly about Karl to his friends at school. Years passed by, and John, now nineteen, still harboured anger and hatred toward his father. One day, to his surprise, Karl visited him and asked to be forgiven, as he had come to realize how much pain he had caused and was sorry for not being there for all those birthdays and Christmases and other holidays. He asked John to forgive him and expressed the desire to build a better relationship now and catch up on the lost time.

Recognizing Karl's sincerity, John's allowed his heart to melt, for in spite of all the anger and resentment, deep down he still loved his father. He instantly forgot years of pain and grief when he realized that Karl still loved him. They now meet on a regular basis and their relationship has been growing in meaningfulness and love. Karl and his ex-wife also have a more respectful relationship and Karl's second wife also is part of the family. They all understand their own roles in the family and live with love and forgiveness.

This is a topical story, as so many children are now raised by single parents, often in situations of great bitterness. Even in the best of divorce scenarios, the child is going to miss the love of the parent who is not there any longer. Children wonder about their own roles in what went wrong. They struggle to understand why they are now deprived of one parent's love. Separation is hard enough for adults and can be heartbreaking for the children involved.

The story of Karl and John illustrates that lost love can be regained if we genuinely forgive others and accept them back into our lives. After all, if God can forgive us, who are we to deny forgiveness to our fellow human beings?

Compassion. Along with kindness and empathy, compassion is among the greatest of soul attributes. We do not instantly acquire compassion. It can develop in one life and return with us in the next, which helps us do more work to grow further in compassion. Life experiences in which we help others in times of crisis are central to our gaining compassion. Compassion flows straight from the heart and not from the mind. There is no connection between our physical minds and compassion—on the contrary, the physical mind resists feeling compassion, which comes from the higher mind and has all the energy and attributes of love. These include selflessness, understanding, patience, and mercy. To be compassionate, we need to have love in our hearts— love for ourselves, for other people, and for the universe. To love is to take the first step toward compassion.

Compassion shows in thoughtful acts. It looks to the best interest of other people. Compassion not only benefits others, but it also serves our own souls. Compassion allows us to emotionally and spiritually enrich the earthly journeys of other souls and ourselves as well. As the Dalai Lama wisely advised, "If you want others to be happy, practice compassion. If you want to be happy, practice compassion."

Temptations and Consciousness

It is very easy to fall prey to temptations. Temptations are the dangling fruits that please the physical mind and body but not the soul. Temptations serve no purpose for our souls. Giving in to them is encouraging evil. The spirit knows what is right and what is wrong, and the spirit will always reject evil, devious, or lustful thoughts. We must therefore resist the cravings of our physical minds.

Temptations come in various forms. Among the most common temptations are those related to money. Some people are greedy and will do anything, good or bad, for money. Others have enough wealth but don't like to share it out of choice and free will to help friends and family who are struggling to make ends meet. But what is the use of wealth when we cannot use it for the well-being of our families and friends? What is the sense in hoarding and multiplying our wealth? Wealth can make us selfish, but it is attractive to our physical minds because we associate it with material comforts and power. We need to remember that the soul does not evolve based on the amount of money we have in our banks, stocks, bonds, and real estate. The soul evolves through acts of love and compassion. Instead of hoarding money, we need to share it out of love with friends and family or donate it to the needy who lack such basic amenities as food, clothing, and shelter in life. The recipients will feel the pure intentions that go with true generosity, love, and compassion.

There is a strong relation between consciousness and how we withstand—or succumb to—temptations. The higher our consciousness, the more likely we are to resist temptations; and the lower our consciousness, the more we are inclined to give in to them. As human beings, we have weaknesses that reside within us. But if our consciousness is awakened or evolved, we are better able to overcome our weaknesses and resist the lure of money and other temptations. The light of consciousness illuminates and helps us control our physical minds. It stops us from exercising our free will to do wrong.

If well-developed, our consciousness is like a best friend—someone who, for our own good, will not hesitate to tell us frankly and openly that what we are doing is wrong. When we make the right, conscious choices in life, the resultant flow of energy is powerful. It satisfies our souls. It fulfills the purpose for which each of us was born, and above all, it takes us forward on the spiritual path of enlightenment and positive transformation.

Aligning Mind, Body, and Spirit
While the physical body is visible and composed of flesh, fluids, and bone, the spiritual body is invisible and made up of energy. The spiritual body resides within the physical body, and they have to be in alignment. The actions and state of one impacts the other. What we think, speak, and act has an impact on our spirits; conversely, the cleaner our spirits, the healthier our physical bodies will be. To keep our spirits clean and pure, we must try to eliminate our negative soul characteristics. It's a gradual but continuous process: remove the negative little by little, step by step; and, one by one, substitute positive qualities.

To lead balanced lives, our minds, bodies and spirits have to be aligned and working in total peace and harmony. A distortion in one aspect changes the channel and frequency of the others. If we are mentally dark and always thinking negative thoughts about others and ourselves, this will impact our physical bodies; and since the soul resides in the physical body, it is also affected. Similarly, our spirits can cause distortions in our physical bodies when we are not walking on the godly, good path. If our actions are selfish, our intentions full of greed and power lust, and our thoughts spiteful and vindictive, our spirits will cause an imbalance in our physical bodies.

Such an imbalance can occur in any part of the physical body, because the flow of energy gets distorted, and pure energy cannot reach the entire body. To realign body, mind, and spirit—to restore balance in our lives—we need to fill the void that exists in our physical minds. We need to fill it with spiritual awareness and the presence and power of God.

This is a matter of being true to ourselves. We need to live simply and selflessly, while having faith and staying connected with the Source. For God will thus guide us in our day-to-day lives and help us maintain the alignment, or harmony, of mind, body, and spirit. When we doubt the Source and his existence, we misalign our spirits and disconnect our souls from the Creator.

This is the biggest possible imbalance that can exist in any human being. The imbalance occurs when we choose to allow our physical minds to dominate our higher minds. The true connection between God and us, his creations, is built on faith and by listening to and strengthening our higher minds. When we choose to let our higher minds take charge, all our actions spring from pure spiritual consciousness. When this happens, we generate peace, tolerance, forgiveness, and compassion. At the same time, we progress in fulfilling the purpose of our earthly births and rebirths: the strengthening of the true self, that spiritual body within each of us—the soul.

• • •

Inspirational Connections

- Your soul is created by, and shares the essence of, God.
- Your soul is immortal; only the body dies.
- The death of the body is necessary for the evolution of your soul.
- You are born and reborn on Earth as part of a divine plan for your spiritual growth through service to other souls.
- For the good of your body and soul, strive to develop positive soul qualities: in particular—peacefulness, tolerance, lovingness, forgivingness, and compassion.
- Your soul always wants to improve, but the physical mind is vulnerable to temptations; guarding against temptations requires making conscious choices.
- Conscious choices depend on keeping your mind, body, and spirit in alignment.
- Maintain alignment through faith, connection to God, and mindfulness of your life's purpose: the improvement of your true self—your eternal soul.

14
Uplifting and Transforming Our Souls

*Let my soul smile through my heart and
my heart smile through my eyes, that I
may scatter rich smiles in sad hearts.*

—Parmahansa Yogananda

THERE ARE VARIOUS WAYS of uplifting and transforming our souls. Each individual selects the method that is best for his or her soul, since consciousness varies from one person to the next. The three most common, direct methods used by those seeking spiritual growth are prayer, meditation, and maintaining silence. In addition to, or as part of these three methods, many people choose to commune with nature on a regular basis—for example, by taking a walk in a park or garden, or by hiking forest or waterfront trails. Each method has one common goal—to sustain and strengthen the soul's connection to God and the universe.

Prayer

No matter where we are born, or which faith we practice in our earthly lives, we are familiar with prayer in some form or another. Above all, prayer is a tool that helps us stay connected with God. Praying is a process that helps us purify our souls and improve spiritually on Earth. Praying helps us distinguish between right and wrong, because it shows us the path of God's light and mercy. Praying removes the negative energy that resides in us and gives us the strength to avoid temptations. Our prayers sustain and guide us as we undergo our tests, training, and suffering on Earth. Prayer helps us to face negative karma as we connect with the divine power and energy of God.

Prayer gives us the confidence that all will be well with us and that we will be helped with our problems. Prayer builds self-esteem and morale as it eliminates our fears and doubts and we start to feel positive about ourselves and our lives. Prayer enforces our faith in times of deepest pain and toughest challenges. It gives us the strength and wisdom to carry on with our daily live. No matter what situation we might find ourselves in, if we pray, we will improve spiritually on Earth.

Prayer has no downside. There are only absolute and positive outcomes from praying, because it puts us in direct communication with God in the most powerful way possible. He listens to all our problems, worries, and doubts; despite our flaws, he gives us blessings and protection. In return, through prayer we show our love for God and offer our ongoing faith and thankfulness for all that we have received in life.

There are no fixed rules for praying. We pray when we want to pray, but each prayer has to be done with honesty, peace, positivity, and total devotion to God Almighty. When we exercise our bodies with full commitment and effort, we achieve maximum results. Much the same is true of praying. Prayer is always helpful, but when we "go the distance" we are that much more improved in spirituality. Pray with positive energy, full faith, sincerity and from the soul and it will guide you to make conscious choices in life. Once guided, follow the path that prayer illuminates.

Prayer is essential nourishment for the soul. Just as we need food to keep our physical bodies energized, we need prayer to charge our spiritual bodies. Even if we have never prayed in our lives, we can start doing so at any time. It is never too late. We always have the ability to add prayer to our daily routines and to thus create powerful positive change in our lives and souls.

Meditation

Meditation is a highly effective and structured tool for disciplining our physical minds. The more we integrate meditation into our day-to-day lives, the more we can control our thoughts, words, and actions. If you practise meditation, you already know that it gives us a peaceful and harmonious feeling, a feeling of contentment prevails in our minds, bodies, and spirits. After meditating, we are energized and inspired to tackle anything and everything that comes our way throughout each day.

Meditating arms us against the hurts that others might inflict on us; it makes pain bearable and frees us from the urge to complain. When loved ones, bosses, or colleagues hurl harsh words at us, the calm of mind that meditation produces gives us the strength not to react. We can smile in the knowledge that this is yet another of life's spiritual tests, and it is not us, but those who speak with negativity and unconsciousness, that are really being harmed. Problems will inevitably come our way, but meditating bolsters the faith and the strength we need to overcome all our hurdles in life. People might bug us, irritate us, taunt us, and ridicule us, but we will practise forbearance and not react to their unconscious barbs. Meditation uplifts the higher mind and controls the physical mind. It diminishes the constant chatter that plays in the physical mind and quells its urgings to return insult for insult, to the detriment of our own souls.

Practising meditation daily is like taking a one-a-day vitamin pill that prevents us from making unconscious choices in life. It makes our higher minds so strong that we can always draw upon the force of positive energy that resides in us. Thus we are likely to make the right choices in life. For each of us, meditation creates awareness of both the true self and the false image that is generated from the ego. Meditation awakens the spirit within each us, and it does so with such force that we feel totally happy, peaceful, exhilarated, and at one with the universe. This feeling can also occur even when we are not in a meditative state. Each episode might last only for a few seconds or minutes, but the overall positive effect on the soul will be permanent. In other words, by putting us in touch with our real selves, meditating contributes to the peace of mind that comes from knowing that, in our spiritual journeys, we are on the godly path of positivity and enlightenment.

I cannot overstress the importance of meditation. I have practised this discipline each day, and I would not think of starting my daily routine without including some dedicated time for meditation. This is a benefit that is free of cost and only requires effort from self and no one else. By its nature, meditation excludes and helps us overcome all our weak and negative feelings and helps us to cultivate positive feelings which are essential for the progression of our soul. The biggest advantage to meditation is that it stops us from reacting to negative situations and destructive people. The self-awareness that meditation fosters enables us to recognize our triggers and thus control our thoughts, words, and actions. For me, meditation has been a God-given blessing. It has helped me to discipline my mind, thoughts, words, and actions; it has made me more patient and calm. Above all else, meditation has shown me the path of forgiveness.

Silence
When we have learned to silence our physical the minds, we have discovered the ultimate secret for accessing our higher minds. When we silence the physical mind, we allow the higher mind to guide us, prompt us, advise us, and provide us with the correct instinct to distinguish between right and wrong and to make conscious choices in life. When we practice silence, we are telling the physical mind to be similarly quiet and to shut down all thoughts, whether they are positive or negative. When we still the clatter of constant undisciplined thoughts, we allow the higher mind to take over and we then feel an awakening of the spirit in each of us.

Through silence, we can see and feel our own flaws. We can grasp where we are wrong in life and how we need to adjust and adapt to make amends to those whom we have hurt. Silence allows us to seek forgiveness on a soul-to-soul level. It allows us to wash away our sins and to forgive our own selves. We thus become the masters of our own selves. Silence teaches us that all of us and each of our individual selves are really one. There is no distinction and there is no division. There is only unity in self and with the universe. Silence teaches us to heal and grow. It teaches us to be humble, caring, and loving toward all human beings on Earth, all living creatures, the environment, and our universe. There is no substitute for silence and if we were to seek it in throughout the universe, we would find it close at hand—deep in our own hearts and souls.

The Role of Nature
Nature offers its own form of silence and provides places and opportunities for prayer and meditation. For nature inspires us with its animals, trees, mountains, lakes, glaciers, plants, flowers, and all the other beauties of Creation. For God is nature and nature is God. If we want to pray, meditate, or seek the silence or solace of our own souls, then we can turn to nature. Even the most callous of callous souls will eventually find something in nature that will resonate in his or her heart. Nature is God's plan for the universe and if we can learn to connect with nature, we can learn to connect with God and other souls on Earth.

Nature is a giver of peace and solace to souls who have lost the right path, but who are struggling to find it again. Nature helps uplift the souls of all those who are willing to explore the spiritual path that leads to God. If, in nature, we can find a moment for prayer, the inspiration to meditate, or the silence that awakens the spirit, then we will be able to find all of these in our own souls. For the soul is connected to nature and to all its healing properties, which are gifts from God.

Avenues to the Soul

Praying, meditating, maintaining silence, and communing with nature—these are pathways by which we stay connected to God. There is nothing more important in any lifetime. At the same time, we must not forget oneness. While our goal is to be at one with the universe and its Creator, we must also remember that, through God, all is connected and interconnected. Thus, the more that we strengthen our connection to God, the more we are aware of our oneness with all other souls.

Finally, we must not neglect the other crucial factor in the great chain of universal connection: the true self—the individual soul. If we neglect our own souls, then our efforts to grow closer to God and to other souls will ultimately be in vain. To progress in uplifting and transforming our souls, we must therefore always look inward to ourselves as spiritual beings. On this imperative rests the immense value of prayer, meditation, silence, and nature. For they are the avenues to the inner person, the true self—the soul. As Swami Vivekananda (1863–1902), an important religious philosopher and Hindu monk, so eloquently expressed it, "You have to grow from the inside out. None can teach you, none can make you spiritual. There is no other teacher but your own soul."

• • •

Inspirational Connections

- You uplift and transform your soul by staying connected to God and the universe.
- You may choose your own method of maintaining the Divine connection.
- The three most common, direct methods are:
    1. Prayer
    2. Meditation
    3. Silence
- Communing with nature inspires prayer, meditation, and silence to uplift your soul.
- Uplifting and transforming your soul begins within yourself.

15
Raising and Shifting Consciousness

*There is no coming to consciousness
without pain. People will do anything,
no matter how absurd, in order to avoid
facing their own soul. One does not become
enlightened by imagining figures of light,
but by making the darkness conscious.*

—Carl Gustav Jung

AS WE PURIFY the spiritual self, the physical self aligns automatically. Conversely, spiritual distortion creates illness or discomfort in the physical body. When something goes wrong with our bodies, we may look for a medical cause alone—for example, virus, disease, allergy, or dietary deficiency. What we often forget is that whether or not there is such a cause for the problem, we should always look inward as well to the state our souls. For the goal to achieve both physical health and progression through life is to keep the soul spiritually clean and pure.

Just as we need to consider that physical health problems have a spiritual component, we must also remember that our negative life experiences do not occur haphazardly. Rather, these experiences come to us so that we learn and grow spiritually. When we think about them solely from our physical minds, however, we tend to become bitter, angry, and irritable; we may feel victimised and let down in life. We blame the circumstances and we blame others but fail to see the fault that lies within us. Until we can grasp what we need to correct spiritually in order to move ahead in life, we will continue to feel scapegoated and targeted by negativity. Raising our consciousness is the key to recognizing the defects in our own souls and the improvements we need to make in both our physical and spiritual lives.

The higher our consciousness, the better will be our spiritual understanding and the more we will be drawn toward spiritual values rather than materialistic things. Consciousness is the path to true happiness, contentment, peace, and fulfillment on Earth. The happiness and contentment that we will discover will touch all other souls that we encounter in our day-to-day lives. The peace that we will find will be the peace for which we have been longing our whole lives but were never before able to experience. And when we have happiness, contentment, and peace, what more is there to desire? As we increasingly come to recognize that life is consciousness, our journeys become inspiring and exciting. We know the true meaning of our lives and appreciate the beauty of all life. We understand why we were born on Earth—to make a difference, by improving our own spirits and, thereby, the lives of others.

Soul Promise

We raise our consciousness by making a promise to our soul to always follow the spiritual path. A soul promise is a commitment made with total honesty and integrity. It is not a promise that we make to another human being on Earth and then break because of the distractions and temptations in our lives. A soul promise is made with free will, total determination, and purity in our bodies, minds, hearts, and spirits. This is a commitment that we make with intent to honour it, no matter what temptations arise in our lives. It is a promise we make in our lives, for our lives, and for our own souls.

A soul promise is not like a resolution that we make in the New Year and then may, or may not, keep. The intent of a soul promise is always pure because we are literally committing to spiritual growth. We only make such a promise when we have reached a point of truly wanting to change our lives, avoid temptations, and eradicate our negative qualities. When we make a soul promise we are determined that, no matter what comes our way, we are willing to accept it, embrace it, and keep moving ahead in life. We are not deterred by any outcome or consequences. We are rock solid and will defy all odds against us. Our willpower is strong, because our goal is to move closer to God—to his spirit, to his knowledge and wisdom, to his radiance and light.

A soul promise is a true gift to the self that cannot be revoked. It can only be kept or broken. Acting solely for personal gain, earthly power, or ego satisfaction is breaking the promise, and this lowers us spiritually. Keeping the promise raises us spiritually because it challenges us. We all have different levels of consciousness, but no matter what we have done in life or how bad our previous acts were, we have the power to change our lives. We have the power to make a promise to our souls and to live by it. When we waver in the face of negative thoughts, challenging situations, and earthly temptations, all we need to do is to have faith in God. When we pray for his guidance, we see the correct path in life and gain the strength to follow it.

We can start the journey with small steps. We can begin with the most modest promise that we can honour, even if it only involves a minor commitment for a single day. But once we have taken that first step—have kept that first soul promise—we will feel different at the end of the day. The difference is that we have inner fulfillment because we have held to the promise and progressed a short way on our own spiritual journey. With our consciousness thus raised, however slightly, we can extend our commitment by making a promise for a week, a month, a year, until finally we reach the stage where we are able to make a promise for life.

When we are truly striving to fulfill a soul promise, the universe will help us. Our higher minds will let us know that we are about to take a wrong step in life and we will feel the pinch in our souls. We will then know that the choices we are about to make are not right for us or for any other person or for the universe as a whole. We will see all our problems in a different light. We will have faith and confidence in ourselves and in our ability to deliver on our promises, for our souls have already evolved to a sufficient degree of consciousness for all this and more to be possible.

Following the Spiritual Path

As we follow the spiritual path, the going will often be tough, rough, and steep. There is no easier route, because there is only one road by which to reach God and that is via our consistent positive actions in life. I have said it many times before and I will say it again, because it is so important: We must forgive all. We must forgive each and every person who will come our way, and who has come our way, defaming, betraying, deceiving, or cheating us in life, and robbing us of our happiness. We need to forgive them for their selfish desires and actions; and most of all, we should forgive them for not having the correct spiritual understanding in life.

Awakening comes to all of us at different stages in life. Some awaken early and follow the spiritual path. Some awaken early, follow the path, and then leave it because it is too rigorous. Some people are just not willing to accept the path until something seriously shakes them up in life. Some people have not found the right path because the environment they are in or the people in their lives are detrimental to their souls, and they fall low spiritually. The wrong relationships or environments can be barriers to moving ahead spiritually. Breakups of couples, families, or friendships are the common results of spiritual misalignment between two souls or among a group of souls. After a period of staying in conflicted relationships or toxic environments, our free will comes into play: we make choices and move out of our troubled relationships and energy-draining environments.

When we are spiritually aligned—that is, moving surely along the path to improvement—we do not hesitate to voice our opinions about wrongs that are being done or injustices being inflicted on others. When we are aligned spiritually, we do not enable our spouses, partners, children, or friends when they choose to go down the wrong path. When we are aligned, we take a firm, or even stern, approach to wrongdoing and those who perpetrate it. People will notice a change in us. Truly aligned people will like and love the spirit we show and will be drawn toward us. People who are misaligned will be afraid of our light and will distance themselves from us. They will feel uncomfortable, powerless, hesitant, or agitated. They will not know how to relate to us.

As we grow in consciousness, we will inevitably face these and other challenges. But the knowledge that we are on the spiritual path is sustaining and guards us against upset. We are aware that more rigorous tests of spirituality are coming our way. While aligned people attract to us, misaligned people move out of our path. Sometimes we might feel lonely in our materialistic world but that feeling lasts only temporarily, for we know at soul level that our true companion is God, and he is with us at every step and turn of our spiritual journeys on Earth.

Shifting Consciousness

The shift in consciousness is happening at different levels of life. Children, students, parents, teachers, employers, employees, managers, and leaders are all involved in furthering this change. Each person or soul is looking for spiritual awareness and development of his or her higher self. The younger generation is not only absorbed in technology but also focused on spiritual growth and development. Many people are making a concerted effort to change their behaviour, to shift consciousness, and to move toward a spiritual destination. They are also trying to inspire others in their journeys on Earth to fulfill their particular dreams and goals. Spiritual consciousness has always been around in some form but, in recent years, has started growing and expanding in many areas of endeavour. At times, many of us may have noticed some level of consciousness in and around us. At other times, we may have been so engrossed in our busy, materialistic day-to-day lives that we failed to notice the spark of consciousness that touched us only yesterday or today or, perhaps, just a moment ago. The very possibility that this may have happened is in itself uplifting.

Awareness comes in different forms and the shift in consciousness happens at different levels depending on the individual, his or her particular soul journey, and the intensity of the higher self. As you, yourself, become spiritually aligned and aware, you will notice the transformation in your own consciousness. When this happens, your thinking and your perception of everything change in the following ways:

1. You become more flexible, selfless, and non-judgemental about people and life.
2. When anger rises in you, it dissolves before it erupts.
3. You prefer peace over arguments and fights, and you humbly walk away from an argument.
4. You notice a change in your own emotions. You become more compassionate, sympathetic, and empathetic to people, the immediate surroundings, and the larger environment.
5. You become more sensitive to other people's troubles and grief. Someone else's problem becomes your problem, and you are ready to jump in and help others out, even though you don't know them.

6. You fight for a just cause.
7. You become humble and are not a show-off. You are drawn toward humility in general.
8. You have a total dislike of manipulation.
9. You see solutions to all your problems.
10. You understand why your friends and loved ones behave or react in particular ways in certain situations.
11. You see the wisdom in every step of your life. You see each day as a blessing for your life, so that you can serve others with your spirit and energy.
12. You love nature—flowers, trees, plants, forests, glaciers, seas, and anything that has a touch of nature.
13. You are true to your spirit. No one can shake or bend you spiritually.
14. You love everyone for their strengths and weaknesses.
15. You provide a helping hand when needed, and you become a pillar of strength for friends, children, and family. People can rely on you.
16. You love yourself ardently and give yourself unconditionally.
17. You value human life and all other life in this universe.
18. You are conscious and selective with your thoughts, words, and actions.
19. You are who you are. You and the self are one.
20. As you change, you find peace and contentment in your life at a soul level, and you inspire others to change with you, including your spouse, children, friends, colleagues, and anyone else that you encounter in your life's journey.

21. You see love in every step of your life and it becomes easy for you to forgive everyone.
22. You will not conspire or intentionally be an instrument in messing up someone's life.
23. You have no fear of job loss, financial troubles, relationship problems, or any other earthly issue that people unnecessarily worry about.
24. You are calm, cool, and patient. Nothing seems to disturb you.
25. Life becomes more joyful and inspiring; most of all, you stay connected with God, minute by minute, hour by hour, and day by day.
26. You love what you do and you love everyone around you with all their flaws.
27. You always carry a strong belief that all will be well and that your life is blessed.
28. You provide meaning to your life and to the lives of others.
29. You are drawn toward creativity, and you spend more time than before engaged in reading, writing, visual arts, crafts, music, and any other endeavour that inspires your soul.
30. You become one with life and the universe, because you are one, and you see yourself and the universe as one, and with this sense of oneness, you lead your daily life.

These are some of the positive and powerful changes that you and, indeed, all of us will experience as we each shift our own consciousness. We all have a quest to discover the purpose of our existence on Earth. As we each become more spiritually enlightened, consciousness is taking a leap forward, bringing about positive change in the existence of other human beings, in the environment, and in the universe.

We can each continue to change for the better, and the resulting collective change emanates outward into the consciousness of the entire universe. Consciousness involves accepting the spiritual truths, speaking the truth, using our power wisely, providing selfless service, directing our energies in a positive and constructive way, building harmonious relationships, and being kind for the betterment of mankind, the environment, and the universe. Consciousness is ignited when we include kindness, compassion, and gratitude in our lives.

Consciousness shifts according to how well we

- lead our lives and uphold the spiritual truths;
- use our energies—thoughts, words, and actions;
- handle our life experiences—tests, training, and soul development;
- build relationships with others;
- treat others—ideally, with respect and dignity;
- understand our journey on Earth; and
- connect with other souls in order to make their earthly journeys pleasant, happy, and peaceful.

Each step expands our spiritual awareness as we make our soul journeys on Earth; each lesson learned lifts us up; each right act draws us closer to pure consciousness; and each good choice brings us nearer to God, our Divine Creator.

The Essence of Life

The essence of all life, including our own, is consciousness. We can only find happiness if we believe in the existence of God, higher mind, soul, and consciousness. Everything else is material fallacy, which will create an illusion of happiness but will leave us empty, shallow, unwanted, and unhappy in our lives. Our conscience is not happy because we have more material wealth. Our conscience can only be happy when we serve others peacefully. Our conscience—that is, the higher mind—raises our own consciousness and once the consciousness is raised, negative thoughts are minimised and positive thoughts are cultivated and implemented. The source of happiness shifts from a material state to a spiritual state, a state where bliss prevails and harmony follows us wherever we go.

The higher our consciousness, the stronger is our soul connection to God; the lower our consciousness, the weaker is our soul connection to God. At the lowest levels of consciousness, we start doubting our faith, and we become arrogant, proud, and rude. There is no other remedy but to change and shift our consciousness—the spiritual awareness that is at the core of our souls.

There is a difference between possessing spiritual knowledge and implementing the knowledge. Possessing the knowledge makes us aware of spirituality and the right thing to do in life. But we can only bring a shift in our own consciousness when we are disciplined, follow the spiritual path in all of life's endeavours, and are not deterred by any obstacles. That is the paradigm shift that each individual must effect in his or her own consciousness. No one can help any of us take this step—we must do it ourselves by our own choice. Once we do so, however, all other spiritual acts in life will come naturally to us as we gradually, but progressively, become more spiritually aligned.

We can only grow in consciousness if we shift our focus and start realizing that we were all born in this universe to help and serve others on Earth. Consciousness is the change that we bring to our lives when we feel a void both in our spirits and earthly surroundings. Consciousness is all about connecting our earthly lives with our higher selves, so that every action we take arises from pure intentions and results in positive outcomes.

On our spiritual journeys, our ultimate companion is God. When we seek his company, he shows us the path, but we must each make our own way along it. And at times this is tough. Some friends will join us in our quest and others will relinquish the friendship. In some cases, spouses and children will remain with us; others will distance themselves from our chosen path.

True spiritual awakening for oneself lies in the self, which cannot be divided. We must not, therefore, worry about other people's actions. We must focus on our own actions and what we can do to improve our souls and spiritual energy. We must think of our own spiritual progress and advancement. When we reach a higher level of consciousness, we do not just need to stay there—we are compelled to strive to move higher still. This means that we cannot allow ourselves to be drawn into temptations, to act unconsciously, and to regress in our spiritual journeys.

When our loved ones cannot, or will not, accompany us on the spiritual path, this is naturally painful for us.

But we have learned that painful experiences can bring realization—that is, correct spiritual understanding. How we view our life experiences is up to us. Sometimes the greatest pain and biggest challenges that we face in our lives end up being our best sources of strength and inspiration for serving others on Earth. When we find that our spiritual progress is distancing us from loved ones, friends, and colleagues, it is helpful to bear in mind the following considerations:

> Everyone's consciousness and learning style is different. People will evolve at their own pace in life.

> We can continue to love those who have yet to find the spiritual path. Love creates love.

> We can—indeed, we should—forgive others' lack of consciousness. Most people are doing the best they can at the point they are at.

> We can create positive energy for ourselves and others by praying and meditating.

> None of us can harm anyone else's spiritual progress. The power to spiritually progress, or regress, lies within each of us and our own souls.

> Life is positive, and the force of positivity will eventually eradicate negativity in life.

Eventually we all have to flow toward the light, elevate our consciousness, and merge with the Creator.

Being the Change

I began this book by writing of the journey that each of us takes in earthly life. At the outset, and throughout the chapters that followed, I emphasized how greatly our individual choices affect our own spiritual growth, the lives of other souls, and the universe as a whole. As this book ends and our journeys continue, I wish you the wisdom to make your choices consciously to bring a change in your consciousness. Your spiritual journey and the desire to change and shift your consciousness is in your own hands. The change is simple - Any thought, word or action that brings pain and misery to any other human being on earth should be avoided at all cost. Any thought, word or action which brings a smile or uplifts the spirit of the other person originates from pure consciousness and is the ideal to which to aspire. Be true to yourself. Listen to the silent but powerful voice of your higher mind and I guarantee that you will raise your consciousness little-by-little and step-by-step. Once you raise your consciousness, you will feel the inner power to take the right step and action in each and every step of your life.

"Be the change you want to see in the world," Mahatma Gandhi (1869–1948) famously said. If our goal is to lead conscious lives in an increasingly conscious world, we should not hesitate to start changing how we as individuals think, behave, interact with others, and manage our daily lives. Our endeavour to shift our own consciousness has the power to inspire others to similarly reach toward higher levels of awareness.

We can all be part of the process of living consciously in peace and harmony, with a view to making the universe a better place for everyone. We can each take the first step of leading our daily lives with positive thoughts, words, and actions. And in this way, collectively, we can bring about a shift in the consciousness of our universe.

The responsibility for positive change lies with each and every soul. Our collective shift in consciousness will be the first inspiring step toward the spiritual improvement of cities, nations, countries, and the universe. The fact that you are reading this book signifies that we were destined to connect in order to help increasing numbers of people live conscious lives. Your decision to raise your own consciousness indicates that our connection did indeed exist previously and that we are reconnected in this life for the purpose of shifting consciousness throughout the universe. Together, we can be the change that we want to see.

• • •

Inspirational Connections

- Consciousness is the key to your physical and spiritual well-being.
- The higher your consciousness, the greater will be your spiritual understanding and personal fulfillment on Earth.
- You raise your consciousness by making a soul promise to follow the spiritual path.
- When you have pure intent and faith in God, the universe helps you keep your soul promise.
- The surest way to stay on the spiritual path is to forgive all who wrong you; forgive them, as they have not yet found the spiritual path.
- Shifting your consciousness to a higher level causes powerful positive changes in yourself, your daily life, and everyone that you encounter.
- Consciousness is the foundation of spiritual living; it is all about connecting your earthly life with your higher mind.
- As you shift consciousness, your loved ones may become distanced from you; if this is painful for you, it helps to remember that, eventually, we all must elevate our own consciousness and become one with God.
- By following the spiritual path and raising your own consciousness, you have the power to create the positive change that you desire in your daily life, on Earth, and in the universe.

Suggested Reading

Bhavnagri, Khorshed. *The Laws of the Spirit World*. 2009. Reprint, Mumbai: Jaico Publishing House, 2011.

Brett, Regina. *God Never Blinks: 50 Lessons for Life's Little Detours*. New York: Grand Central Publishing, 2011.

Brinkley, Dannion. *Saved by the Light: The True Story of a Man Who Died Twice*.... With Paul Perry. Introduction by Raymond Moody, MD. 1994. New York: HarperCollins, 2008.

Cayce, Edgar. *A Search for God*. Books 1 and 2. 1942. Reprint, [Virginia Beach]: Edgar Cayce Foundation, 2013.

Chopra, Deepak. *The Seven Spiritual Laws of Success: A Practical Guide to the Fulfillment of Your Dreams*. 1994. Reprint, New Delhi: Excel Books, 1997.

Easwaran, Eknath, trans. *The Bhagavad Gita*. 2nd ed. Tomales, CA: Nilgiri Press (Blue Mountain Center of Meditation), 2007.

———. *The Upanishads*. 2nd ed. Tomales, CA: Nilgiri Press (Blue Mountain Center of Meditation), 2007.

Kushner, Harold S. *When Bad Things Happen to Good People*. Toronto: Random House of Canada, 1981.

Mundy, Jon, PhD. *Living "A Course in Miracles": An Essential Guide to the Classic Text*. New York: Sterling Ethos. 2011.

Singer, Michael A. *The Untethered Soul: The Journey beyond Yourself*. Oakland, CA: New Harbinger Publications, 2007.

Tolle, Eckhart. *A New Earth: Awakening to Your Life's Purpose*. New York: Penguin / Plume, 2006.

Zukav, Gary. *The Seat of the Soul*. 25th anniversary edition. New York: Simon & Schuster Paperbacks, 2014.

• • •

Author Biography

Nozer Kanga is a lifelong student of karma, spirituality, and consciousness. His spiritual journey began in Mumbai, India, where he studied with Khorshed Bhavnagri, the author of *The Laws of the Spirit World*.

Kanga's own book, *Living with Consciousness*, is the result of years of extensive research, hard-won insight, and life experience.

Kanga currently resides in North Vancouver, British Columbia, Canada.

Made in the USA
Columbia, SC
25 April 2018